Top Careers in Two Years

Construction and Trades

Titles in the *Top Careers in Two Years* Series

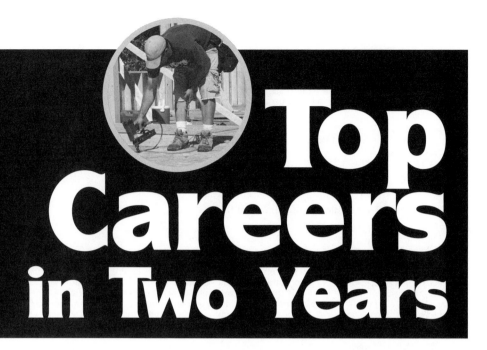

Top Careers in Two Years

Construction and Trades

Deborah Porterfield

Ferguson Publishing
An imprint of Infobase Publishing

Top Careers in Two Years
Construction and Trades

Ferguson
An imprint of Infobase Publishing
132 West 31st Street
New York, NY 10001

ISBN-13: 978-0-8160-6897-5
ISBN-10: 0-8160-6897-6

Library of Congress Cataloging-in-Publication Data

Top careers in two years.
   v. cm.
   Includes index.
   Contents: v. 1. Food, agriculture, and natural resources / by Scott Gillam — v. 2. Construction and trades / Deborah Porterfield — v. 3. Communications and the arts / Claire Wyckoff — v. 4. Business, finance, and government administration / Celia W. Seupal — v. 5. Education and social services / Jessica Cohn — v. 6. Health care, medicine, and science / Deborah Porterfield — v. 7. Hospitality, human services, and tourism / Rowan Riley — v. 8. Computers and information technology / Claire Wyckoff — v. 9. Public safety, law, and security / Lisa Cornelio, Gail Eisenberg — v. 10. Manufacturing and transportation — v. 11. Retail, marketing, and sales / Paul Stinson.
   ISBN-13: 978-0-8160-6896-8 (v. 1 : hc : alk. paper)
   ISBN-10: 0-8160-6896-8 (v. 1 : hc : alk. paper)
   ISBN-13: 978-0-8160-6897-5 (v. 2 : hc. : alk. paper)
   ISBN-10: 0-8160-6897-6 (v. 2 : hc. : alk. paper)
   ISBN-13: 978-0-8160-6898-2 (v. 3 : hc : alk. paper)
   ISBN-10: 0-8160-6898-4 (v. 3 : hc : alk. paper)
   ISBN-13: 978-0-8160-6899-9 (v. 4 : hc : alk. paper)
   ISBN-10: 0-8160-6899-2 (v. 4 : hc : alk. paper)
   ISBN-13: 978-0-8160-6900-2 (v. 5 : hc : alk. paper)
   ISBN-10: 0-8160-6900-X (v. 5 : hc : alk. paper)
   ISBN-13: 978-0-8160-6901-9 (v. 6 : hc : alk. paper)
   ISBN-10: 0-8160-6901-8 (v. 6 : hc : alk. paper)
   ISBN-13: 978-0-8160-6902-6 (v. 7 : hc : alk. paper)
   ISBN-10: 0-8160-6902-6 (v. 7 : hc : alk. paper)
   ISBN-13: 978-0-8160-6903-3 (v. 8 : hc : alk. paper)
   ISBN-10: 0-8160-6903-4 (v. 8 : hc : alk. paper)
   ISBN-13: 978-0-8160-6904-0 (v. 9 : hc : alk. paper)
   ISBN-10: 0-8160-6904-2 (v. 9 : hc : alk. paper)
   ISBN-13: 978-0-8160-6905-7 (v. 10 : hc : alk. paper)
   ISBN-10: 0-8160-6905-0 (v. 10 : hc : alk. paper)
   ISBN-13: 978-0-8160-6906-4 (v. 11 : hc : alk. paper)
   ISBN-10: 0-8160-6906-9 (v. 11 : hc : alk. paper)
   1. Vocational guidance—United States. 2. Occupations—United States. 3. Professions—United States.
   HF5382.5.U5T677 2007
   331.7020973—dc22

                          2006028638

Ferguson books are available at special discounts when purchased in bulk quantities for businesses, associations, institutions, or sales promotions. Please call our Special Sales Department in New York at (212) 967-8800 or (800) 322-8755.

You can find Ferguson on the World Wide Web at http://www.fergpubco.com

Produced by Print Matters, Inc.
Text design by A Good Thing, Inc.
Cover design by Salvatore Luongo

Printed in the United States of America

Sheridan PMI 10 9 8 7 6 5 4 3 2

This book is printed on acid-free paper.

Contents

How to Use This Book

This book, part of the *Top Careers in Two Years* series, highlights in-demand careers for readers considering a two-year degree program—either straight out of high school or after working a job that does not require advanced education. The focus throughout is on the fastest-growing jobs with the best potential for advancement in the field. Readers learn about future prospects while discovering jobs they may never have heard of.

An associate's degree can be a powerful tool in launching a career. This book tells you how to use it to your advantage, explore job opportunities, and find local degree programs that meet your needs.

Each chapter provides the essential information needed to find not just a job but a career that fits your particular skills and interests. All chapters include the following features:

- "Vital Statistics" provides crucial information at a glance, such as salary range, employment prospects, education or training needed, and work environment.

- Discussion of salary and wages notes hourly versus salaried situations as well as potential benefits. Salary ranges take into account regional differences across the United States.

- "Keys to Success" is a checklist of personal skills and interests needed to thrive in the career.

- "A Typical Day at Work" describes what to expect at a typical day on the job.

- "Two-Year Training" lays out the value of an associate's degree for that career and what you can expect to learn.

- "What to Look For in a School" provides questions to ask and factors to keep in mind when selecting a two-year program.

- "The Future" discusses prospects for the career going forward.

- "Interview with a Professional" presents firsthand information from someone working in the field.

- ⚷ "Job Seeking Tips" offers suggestions on how to meet and work with people in the field, including how to get an internship or apprenticeship.

- ⚷ "Career Connections" lists Web addresses of trade organizations providing more information about the career.

- ⚷ "Associate's Degree Programs" provides a sampling of some of the better-known two-year schools.

- ⚷ "Financial Aid" provides career-specific resources for financial aid.

- ⚷ "Related Careers" lists similar related careers to consider.

In addition to a handy comprehensive index, the back of the book features two appendices providing invaluable information on job hunting and financial aid. Appendix A, Tools for Career Success, provides general tips on interviewing either for a job or two-year program, constructing a strong résumé, and gathering professional references. Appendix B, Financial Aid, introduces the process of applying for aid and includes information about potential sources of aid, who qualifies, how to prepare an application, and much more.

Introduction

Construction jobs and the trades (automotive repair, marine technician, and aircraft mechanic) are all careers that never go out of style. Even when the economy is in a downturn, buildings are still being constructed or renovated, and cars, planes, and boats need repairs. Look around at your neighborhood, and you'll probably notice construction happening on homes, hospitals, schools, highways, malls, and other structures. Nearly 7 million people work in construction today and the industry needs about 240,000 new workers each year, according to 2006 information from TryTools, the career site of Associated Builders and Contractors (http://www.abc.org).

According to the Bureau of Labor Statistics, most construction workers are employed full time and many work more than 40 hours a week. Because jobs often must be completed on deadline, these skilled workers put in time on the weekends, evenings, and holidays. They usually work in all types of weather as well. The work is very physical and there is a certain amount of danger handling power tools or heavy equipment, sometimes using them at great heights. Most construction businesses are small, employing fewer than 20 workers, and construction workers are often self-employed, as the chart on this page demonstrates.

Many constructions occupations have a substantial percentage of self-employed workers:

Painters and paperhangers	45.5 percent
Carpet, floor, and tile installers and finishers	41.6 percent
Carpenters	33.1 percent
Brick mason, block masons, and stonemasons	30.1 percent
Roofers	25.5 percent
Drywall installers, ceiling tile installers, and tapers	22.1 percent
Plumbers and related careers	13.2 percent
Insulation workers	10.0 percent
Electricians	3.7 percent

Source: The Bureau of Labor Statistics

Opportunities in construction are very varied, as you will see reading through this volume—whether you want to help the general public by working on civil engineering projects like highways or airports or if you're very artistically inclined and want to design offices as an interior decorator. All jobs share a common love of working with hands and equipment to solve problems and improve people's lives. Plus, materials and techniques for building keep changing, so tradespeople have to stay up to date.

Some construction workers who excel at communications, organization, and handling people advance into managerial positions. Employers often require supervisors to have more college education than a two-year degree, but an associate's degree is a solid starting place. These positions include assistant manager, construction manager, general superintendent, cost estimator, construction building inspector, general manager, or top executive, contractor, or consultant. Business courses can be a definite asset in these jobs as well.

We could only cover a sampling of construction careers in this volume. Others you may want to explore are construction equipment operator; metal worker; drywall and ceiling tile installer; plasterer; segmental paver; terrazzo worker; painter and paperhanger; glazier; roofer; carpet, floor, and tile installer; insulation worker; and sheet metal worker. A few other related careers are elevator installer, demolition expert, and trucker (a person who delivers and unloads building materials).

Construction projects are expected to increase over the next decade, especially in booming areas in the South and West. More condominiums are going up in urban areas as home hunters search for more affordable options. The construction of nursing homes and health care facilities is expected to rise as well as the population ages. Remodeling is bigger than ever and opportunities are swelling as homeowners continue to pursue remodeling projects.

Opportunities are expected to be very good for auto, marine, and aircraft technicians as well. Mechanics with diagnostic and problem-solving skills, knowledge of electronics and mathematics, and mechanical aptitude should fare very well. Staying up to date with technology is crucial in this field as electronics and computer components keep becoming more sophisticated. Automotive mechanics, for example, must understand the integrated electronic systems and complex computers that make vehicles operate. Technicians must increasingly build a broad base of knowledge about how vehicles' complex components interact and how to use electronic diagnostic equipment and computer-based technical reference materials to solve problems.

Basic duties for mechanics are to inspect, maintain, and repair. They need to have stamina and love working with their hands, using hand tools to solve most problems. Marine, aircraft, and auto technicians all know how engines operate. Handheld diagnostic computers are often vital for pinpointing engine trouble. An important job for mechanics is to keep parts well maintained and lubricated before they break. Often, they replace old parts to make sure there is no equipment failure later on when a person is operating a vehicle.

The previous term for mechanic was *grease monkey*, and it made sense. This is a job where you a have move in all sorts of positions like a monkey and you definitely get dirty and greasy. Courses that help mechanics are engine repair, electronics, physics, chemistry, English, computers, and mathematics.

Related mechanic careers not in this volume are diesel truck mechanic and motorcycle mechanic.

The Two-Year/Apprenticeship Combination

Many tradespeople learn their craft by combining a two-year degree program with an apprenticeship. Sometimes there is no availability for students to enter an apprenticeship program right away, but they can get started earning a two-year degree to become an electrician or carpenter or another tradesperson. Many apprentices complete their general education courses and receive associate's degrees in their trade. Apprenticeships provide hands-on training through local employers, trade associations, and trade unions, and combine that work with classroom instruction.

Although finishing an apprenticeship can take five to six years, apprentices are on the job earning a paycheck. Apprentices not only earn wages but also health benefits and a pension. Those starting to apprentice as an electrician in Illinois earn about $15 an hour. That wage more than doubles as the apprentice works up to journeyman status. A typical electrician apprenticeship program consists of 6,000 hours of on-the-job training by union electrical contractors and a minimum of 540 hours of related classroom instruction. Also, some companies seek graduates from two-year programs for their supervisory positions.

Community colleges often combine apprenticeships and coursework. For example, Honolulu Community College coordinates all construction apprenticeship training for the island of Oahu, and has certificate and associate's degree programs in Applied Trades, Carpentry Technology, Architecture, Engineering and Computer-Assisted Design, Electrical Installation and Maintenance Technology, Occupational and Environmental Safety Management, Refrigeration and Air Conditioning Technology, Sheet Metal and Plastics Technology, and Welding Technology.

Benefits of an Associate's Degree

For someone who doesn't want to devote four years to college, or can't afford it, a smart alternative is to get an associate's degree, which can lead straight to work. The associate's degree also can be a steppingstone to a bachelor's degree later on—if you decide you need one. For millions of Americans, associate's degrees provide the essential training needed to pursue a rewarding career without the expense of a four-year degree. The U.S. Department of Education's National Center for Education Statistics estimates that by the end of 2005, more than 6.1 million students will have enrolled in degree-granting two-year institutions. The number of associate's degrees conferred continues to increase each year.

Compared with those who hold only a high school degree, associate's-degree holders earn more money ($2,000–$6,000 a year more on average) and face a much lower rate of unemployment. Also, consider that 43 percent of four-year college graduates are underemployed. On the other hand, there's a shortage of people with technical skills, including those who train at the two-year level. Another plus: The average annual tuition and fees for 2005–06 at a four-year private college was $21,235, while the annual cost at a public two-year institution averaged $2,191, according to latest statistics from the College Board. And financial aid is not just for four-year college students—those attending trade, technical, vocational, two-year, and career colleges can also qualify for aid. See Appendix B for information on financial aid .

"A four-year degree is a ticket to get in line for an oversold airplane," says Kenneth C. Gray, a professor of workforce education and development at Penn State University. But for two-year degree holders, "There's more seats on the airplane than people holding tickets." A degree can be very useful in business, but work experience and solid skills, even for degreed individuals, are also highly valued.

Flexibility is one of the main attractions of two-year degrees. Classes are often offered at night, close to home, and on the Internet. (However, don't be scammed—be sure to check out *accreditation* under "Finding the Right School.") Those looking for the more traditional college experience will find that at least 20 percent of two-year colleges provide housing, cafeterias, sports, clubs, and a bustling social scene.

Another great feature of associate's degree programs is that admission is not overly competitive. Students are admitted from a wide range of academic backgrounds. So someone who performed below average in high school can excel at a two-year school if they put in the time and energy.

Just because you earn a two-year degree does not mean your education has to stop there. Many who start with a two-year degree continue on with their higher education, pursuing a four-year degree and often transferring credits earned from their two-year program. (When you investigate two-year programs, find out if your credits will be transferable or not before you sign on the dotted line.) Some even go on to earn a more advanced professional degree. Often, if you pursue academics directly related to your job, your employer will pay some or all of your tuition.

Are Construction and the Trades for You?

Ask yourself the following questions to see if the careers in this book might be right for you.

Do you enjoy working with your hands?

Do you like variety in your work?

Are you dependable (you've missed very few day of school
or another job)?

Is physical work important to you?

Do you think you could handle working in all types of weather?

Do you enjoy working with tools?

Can you get along with different types of personalities?

Are you a good problem solver?

Do you hate the idea of a desk job?

Do you like seeing the direct results of your labor at the end
of the day?

Are you dedicated to finishing projects?

Are you good at working independently without a boss looking
over your every move?

Do you have solid math skills?

Do you thrive in a team environment?

If you answered "yes" to most of these, then construction or the trades
may be for you.

Finding the Right School

Two-year colleges abound, and there may be one close to home. Even so,
don't dive into the closest college program without doing some research
first. It is important to review different schools to understand what your
local college may and may not offer. There might be another local school
better suited to your interests, or you might decide to go away to school
and live with relatives, a friend, or in a dormitory.

A good place to begin your search for the right two-year college is online
at http://www.collegeboard.com. You can create a profile of exactly what
kind of school and program you want, in whatever location you want, and
see which colleges come up. Another good place to begin your search is in
the library; most libraries carry college directories and many individual cat-
alogues. Be sure to investigate each college that looks interesting with a
search of the college's Web site, a review of their catalogue, and a chat with
someone at the school.

Whatever college you choose, make sure that it is accredited by one of
the agencies recognized by the U.S. Department of Education. Be aware
that some "colleges" may appear legitimate but might not be accredited or
recognized by the U.S. Department of Education. Don't go through all that
hard work and end up with a nonaccredited degree! You can check
"Diploma Mills and Accreditation" at the U.S. Department of Education's
Web site: http://www.ed.gov/students/prep/college/diplomamills/index.html;

more information is available at the Council for Higher Education Accreditation: http://www.chea.org.

The following are top accrediting agencies.

Regional and National Accrediting Agencies Recognized by the U.S. Department of Education

✔ Accrediting Council for Independent Colleges and Schools
✔ Distance Education and Training Council
✔ Middle States Association of Colleges and Schools
✔ New England Association of Schools and Colleges
✔ North Central Association of Colleges and Schools
✔ Northwest Association of Schools and Colleges
✔ Southern Association of Colleges and Schools
✔ Western Association of Schools and Colleges

More Info

For general information on jobs in the construction industry, contact:

✔ Associated Builders and Contractors, Workforce Development Department, 9th Floor, 4250 North Fairfax Drive, Arlington, VA 22203.   http://www.trytools.org
✔ Associated General Contractors of America, Inc., 2300 Wilson Boulevard, Suite 400, Arlington, VA 22201.   http://www.agc.org
✔ National Association of Home Builders, Home Builders Institute, 1201 15th Street, NW, Washington, DC 20005-2800. http://www.hbi.org
✔ National Center for Construction Education and Research, P.O. Box 141104, Gainesville, FL, 32614.   http://www.nccer.org
✔ Automotive Jobs Today, 8400 Westpark Drive, MS #2, McLean, VA 22102.   http://www.autojobstoday.org
✔ Career Voyages, U.S. Department of Labor, 200 Constitution Avenue, NW, Washington DC 20210.   http://www.careervoyages.gov/automotive-main.cfm
✔ Aircraft Mechanics Fraternal Association, Suite 208 A, 67 Water Street, Laconia, NH 03246.   http://www.amfanatl.org

Carpenter

Vital Statistics

Salary: Carpenters earn on average about $17 an hour—which would mean an annual rate of $35,000, except weather often slows construction work below the supply of available workers, according to 2006 data from the U.S. Bureau of Labor Statistics.

Employment: There are approximately 1.2 million carpentry jobs in the United States. More than half of these jobs are with contractors. Twelve percent of carpenters work in heavy construction and nearly one third are self-employed. Carpentry jobs are expected to increase about as fast as the average for all jobs through 2014.

Education: Many associate of arts (AA) and associate of applied science (AAS) degrees can be completed in 18 months. In addition to hands-on experience, carpentry students take classes in construction safety, tools and materials, concrete forms and footings, reading blueprints, framing and stair building, furniture making, as well as a liberal arts class or two.

Work Environment: Indoors and outdoors. Work locations are likely to change throughout the year.

Do you like to build shelves, backyard fences, or tree houses? Is *This Old House* one of your favorite TV shows? If so, you could find yourself making kitchen cabinets, remodeling a school, or building a bridge. Most people know that carpenters play a major role in home and commercial construction, but did you know that carpentry skills also can be applied to building maintenance and furniture repair? Wood is the material carpenters typically work with, but some carpenters replace windows and others install industrial machinery. There are more carpenters in the construction industry than in any other trade, and carpenters work almost everywhere in the country.

Outside the construction industry, carpenters build sets for movies, TV shows, and theaters; change locks and do handy work for office complexes; set up and break down trade shows; and craft wooden boats, to name a few of the special niches carpenters have carved out for themselves.

Carpentry is physical work, but there are tasks in which attention to detail is more important than physical strength. Finish work is one such area in which many women carpenters choose to specialize. Finish work includes putting the trim around doors and windows, molding, and the baseboard just above the floor—it is prominently visible and requires precise measurements.

When building and remodeling residential homes, carpenters frame walls, put up drywall, install windows and doors, and restore existing woodwork. On commercial sites, carpenters may pour concrete, put up scaffolds, and build bracing for structures. The skills needed to perform a wide range of tasks are interchangeable, so that carpenters can move from residential to commercial and back depending on the location of the work.

> ## "The carpenter is not the best who makes more chips than all the rest."
> —Arthur Guiterman, American humorist

On the Job

Carpenters work with a wide range of handheld and power tools, including hammers, screwdrivers, hand saws, drills, table saws, and miter saws. Carpentry is physically demanding. Tools and materials must be unloaded and carried to the work area. Cutting and assembling materials, even with the help of power tools, takes a lot of energy. Sometimes equipment and materials have to be carried up ladders or put on lifts. In construction, it is helpful for carpenters to have good balance and not be afraid of heights. This is much less of a concern for carpenters who pursue fields such as furniture building or instrument making.

Construction carpenters frequently must kneel or stand for hours at a time. They also may have to spend much or all of their day working outside in cold, wet, or hot conditions. Even inside, it can be cold and damp on some jobs. Bad weather may temporarily halt a construction project that could translate into lost wages for carpenters.

Although safety is a priority on most job sites, injuries from falls or power tools can keep carpenters from working. Another risk factor is hearing loss due to noise from heavy equipment and power tools on the site, but protective hearing devices can be worn to minimize this risk.

Nevertheless, many carpenters would much prefer to deal with bad weather at times and be physically exhausted at the end of the day than sit for eight hours behind a desk.

Keys to Success

To be a successful carpenter, you should have

➤ physical strength and stamina

➤ eye–hand coordination

- ⚷ manual dexterity
- ⚷ good balance
- ⚷ math skills
- ⚷ communication skills

Do You Have What It Takes?

It's important to know going into this career that you will depend on your knowledge of math, and you will probably have to learn more math to complete your two-year degree in carpentry. Carpenters must learn how to read blueprints or plans and understand how to apply local building codes to construction projects.

Carpenters should enjoy constant physical work and working with their hands. On the job, carpenters sometimes work independently, and other times they will work on a team. Adaptability is also important as working conditions change routinely. Because a growing number of construction workers across the country do not speak English, Spanish language skills are valued, particularly for those who want to become supervisors. Even if that is not your goal, the ability to communicate clearly on job sites can be a valuable skill for a carpenter.

A Typical Day at Work

On large job sites, carpenters often get instructions from their supervisors at the beginning of the day. At some point, they also check and recheck the blueprints. Blueprints outline how large a structure is to be as well as the type and size of materials needed to build it. These materials have to be cut or shaped, and then put together to build that structure. After materials are measured and marked, carpenters nail, screw, or glue them together, using levels and other measuring devices to check their work. A carpenter may do this alone or with other carpenters. At the end of the day, tools and materials must be left in such a way that they will not be dangerous to workers returning to the site the next day. Carpenters who are self-employed may work entirely on their own or with a helper or two.

How to Break In

If you are thinking of going straight to work as a carpenter with no training, think again. Apprentices can learn the trade while earning a paycheck, and they usually earn more right from the start than those who walk onto a construction site and take a job. Apprentices learn quickly and thoroughly in formal, structured educational programs that combine classroom study with on-the-job experience. Some apprenticeship programs, such as the one sponsored by the United Brotherhood of Carpenters (UBC) (http://www.carpenters.org/), provide health insurance. UBC apprentices also work toward retirement benefits. The salary of an apprentice goes up in stages as he or she progresses in the program. Like most others in the workforce, apprentices work year round.

Building a solid skill base is the best insurance carpenters have for finding the next job after one project finishes. Without this basic training, less skilled carpenters may be passed over in favor of carpenters who have a solid foundation in the fundamentals.

Two-Year Training

While an associate's degree in carpentry can take two years to earn, it may take an additional two years to complete apprenticeship work and begin working as a full-fledged carpenter. Apprenticeships combined with associate's degree programs eventually lead to journeyman status. Becoming a journeyman means a carpenter has reached a highly skilled level, at which point he or she can join a carpenter's union, securing higher wages, union health insurance, further training, and assistance finding employment.

An apprenticeship with the UBC takes 8,000 hours and about four years to complete. Apprentices periodically spend a week in the classroom and the rest of their time on an actual job site. Community college degree programs start with more classroom training before students move into the apprenticeship phase. Participants in an apprenticeship program must be at least 18 years old, whereas students in a carpentry program at a community college can start at a younger age.

A good way to prepare in high school is to take preapprenticeship or vocational carpentry and construction classes. If your high school does not offer vocational training, courses in algebra, geometry, physics, and mechanical drawing can help you get off to a solid start. Because communications skills are valued in this field, it's smart to take English and Spanish as well.

In hands-on training, students and apprentices begin to master manual and power tools, applying basic construction techniques to wood and other construction materials. As they learn how buildings are designed and how to stay safe on the job, carpenters-in-training gain an understanding of their role in the construction process and how they interact with other construction tradespeople such as plumbers, roofers, and electricians.

What to Look For in a School

Here are some things to think about when choosing a two-year school:

☞ Which school in your area offers exactly what you want to learn? Is there a program that has a better reputation or teaches what you are looking for in the next town?

☞ Will the school provide enough hands-on training to go straight to work after completing the program? Try to visit the school's facilities and talk to the instructors before committing yourself to the program.

☞ Does the trade school or community college require that you pass a standardized placement test, such as the COMPASS (http://www.act.org/compass/index.html), when you apply for admission? This test helps determine what level math and English classes best suit each student.

☞ How long does it take the program's graduates generally to find a job? Do all of the graduates find carpentry work?

☞ What are the program's specialty areas? Keep in mind that you might think you know what you want to learn to do, but after some experience, you might want to specialize in another area of carpentry. It's nice to have options.

☞ Did the instructors work as carpenters in the field before they started teaching?

To see how you like carpentry before investing time and money in a program, consider volunteering for Habitat for Humanity or other community service building projects in your area. Volunteer construction projects also could take you to other countries if you want a vocational study experience abroad to be part of your education.

The Future

With the baby boomer generation retiring, opportunities for carpenters entering the field will remain steady and are expected to grow. Regions experiencing population growth have a greater need for carpenters. With carpentry skills, you can usually find work in other regions temporarily or longer term if the construction market slows down in the area in which you are living.

Job Seeking Tips

See the suggestions below and look in Appendix A for advice on writing your first résumé, preparing for your first school and job interviews, and who to ask for references.

✔ Attend career workshops and information sessions at your school.

✔ Listen to what your vocational instructors say about looking for work and ask them about the course of their careers.

✔ While getting a basic carpentry education, ask yourself what you like doing best. Consider specializing in those areas.

Interview with a Professional:
Q&A

Meg Steere

Carpenter, Seattle, Washington

Q: *How did you get started?*

A: After college I went into graphic design for Web sites—it was during the dot-com era. Although the creative part was great, sitting all day at a computer was torture. It just wasn't active enough for me. I spent the next couple of years trying to figure out what I wanted to do career-wise. A friend told me about the woodworking program and I decided to apply.

On my first day of the program, the instructor said that the students in this program come from all kinds of backgrounds, but the one thing they all have in common is that they love working with their hands. At that moment, I knew I was in the right place.

Q: *What's a typical day like?*

A: I started out working for a remodeling company and then decided to go out on my own. I buy houses that need fixing up, completely remodel them, and then sell the house. I manage the project and do a lot of the work. The night before, I plan what I am going to do the next day. I like to get going early and am usually on the job site by 7:45 or 8:00 a.m. There are a variety of things I do on a given day. They can range from framing for walls, to putting up joists or rafters, to adding trim to the interior of the house. On my houses, I end up doing more than just carpentry—the other day I dug a ditch out to the water main so the plumber could lay pipe.

I want to know how to do it all—how to build a house from the ground up, and I am still learning lots! Learning something new every day and seeing how it all comes together in the process of rebuilding a house keeps my interest. It is very physical work—by the end of the day I am worn out for sure.

Q: *What's your advice for those starting a career?*

A: I'm happy I went into an educational program where the first thing we learned was how to use all the tools safely. I also got a foundation in all aspects of carpentry and saw what areas I liked better and wanted to go into. I would encourage students to choose a program they can afford, as opposed to rushing into the field right away. If you go to work right away, most likely you will start as a laborer, which means doing the grunt work like carrying wood or hauling trash.

(continued on next page)

(continued from previous page)

As a carpenter, you are working around really loud machinery and tools that can hurt you. Take precautions that are easy to take, such as wearing safety goggles and hearing protection. You see a lot of people acting tough and saying they don't need to take these precautions, but it's a smart thing to do. I am very glad I got a strong background in safety in the woodworking program—it has definitely made a difference in how I approach things.

Q: *What's the best part of being a carpenter?*

A: My job is really wide ranging—from roofing to working on the siding, and there is a lot of variety in between. After a few days on one project, I move on to another part of the house. I like the variety carpentry offers. Some other jobs are the same thing day after day, and that gets pretty old.

There also seems to be a universal need for carpenters. As soon as I say I am a carpenter, people tell me about the work that needs to be done on their house. There seems to be a lot to do and a lot of opportunity out there.

Did You Know?

The actor Harrison Ford and Larry Wachowski, the director of *The Matrix*, started out as carpenters. Tom Silva, the host of the TV show *This Old House*, has been doing carpentry projects since he was a kid.

Career Connections

For more information contact the following organizations.

United Brotherhood of Carpenters and Joiners of America
http://www.carpenters.org

Home Builders Institute http://www.buildingcareers.org

Residential Carpenter Contractors Association
http://www.ceacisp.org

Associate's Degree Programs

Here are a few schools with two-year carpentry programs:

Seattle Central Community College, Seattle, Washington

Bakersfield College, Bakersfield, California

St. Louis Community College, Forest Park, Missouri

State University of New York College of Technology, Delhi, New York
Austin Community College, Austin, Texas
John A. Logan College, Carterville, Illinois

Financial Aid

Here is one source that provides carpentry-related scholarships. For more on financial aid for two-year students, turn to Appendix B. Note that construction scholarships often are state based. Ask your community college or technical school to refer you to the local builders associations that provide assistance for students enrolled in two-year degree programs.

United Brotherhood of Carpenters and Joiners of America
Local union branches often offer financial awards for carpenter apprentices. Contact your local union.   http://www.carpenters.org

Related Careers

Roofer, stone mason, bricklayer, window and door fabricator, architectural drafter, metal worker, exterminator, fencer, structural engineer, painter, surveyor, intercom/doorbell installer, carpet installer, construction and building inspector, drywall and ceiling tile installer, taper, tile and marble setter, and heating and air conditioning mechanics and installer.

Plumber

Vital Statistics

Salary: The median hourly wage is $19.85 with an annual salary of more than $41,000. Highly skilled plumbers can earn more than $70,000 a year, according to 2006 data from the U.S. Bureau of Labor Statistics.

Employment: The demand for plumbers is high and is expected to grow about as fast as avergae for all occupations through 2014.

Education: An associate's degree and an apprenticeship provide solid preparation for a plumbing career. Key classroom subjects include drafting, mathematics, and blueprint reading.

Work Environment: Depending on the job, a plumber may work indoors or outdoors and in residential or commercial settings.

Many people think of a plumber as the "lifesaver" who comes to the rescue when a pipe bursts or a drain clogs. While such emergency tasks are important, skilled plumbers also perform many other vital duties. They install the plumbing systems that carry water, waste, and gas through pipes in homes, schools, stores, and factories. They also install the bathroom sinks, toilets, water heaters, and other plumbing fixtures that make modern life so comfortable. Some plumbers also use their knowledge of building codes and plumbing systems to help design new buildings.

On high-end projects, plumbers sometimes get to install luxurious projects with a high-tech twist. Depending on what a customer wants and can afford, a plumber might install a whirlpool with a built-in sound system, set up a versatile shower system with a 10-button control panel, and put in a thermostat-controlled toilet with a heated seat and built-in dryer.

Even though plumbing is one of the best paid careers in construction, with top earners making more than $70,000 a year, not enough people are going into the field, so the employment outlook for plumbers continues to be excellent.

To become a successful plumber, you need to be good at math, enjoy working with your hands, and be strong enough to lift heavy pipes. Knowing how to communicate with customers, contractors, and colleagues also is important.

High school students who are interested in pursuing a career in plumbing can get a head start by signing up for courses in plane geometry, shop, physics, English, and speech.

Once a student finishes high school, he or she is ready to start a two-year degree program that offers plumbing-related courses, such as blueprint reading, drafting, mathematics, and mechanical drawing. The best college programs also help students find apprenticeships that provide on-the-job training. Students who work as apprentices are paid while they learn. Generally they start at a rate that's about half that of experienced plumbers. As their skills increase, so do their wages. At the end of an apprenticeship, a plumber can become a journeyman who is recognized as a skilled craftsman and eligible for higher-paying jobs.

As a plumber, you will have the opportunity to pursue different career paths: Some plumbers specialize in home repairs and maintenance, traveling from site to site throughout the day. Others use their plumbing skills to keep the water, waste, and heat flowing in commercial buildings, such as shopping malls, colleges, and factories. Some plumbers work in construction, designing and installing plumbing systems for new buildings. A plumber who passes a master plumber's examination can start his or her own business and work as an independent contractor.

Many workers in the plumbing field specialize in specific areas. A pipe layer, for example, lays pipes for drains, water mains, sewers, and oil and gas lines. A pipe fitter installs, fixes, and regulates pipe systems that are used to manufacture products, heat and cool buildings, and make electricity. Some specialize even further. A steam fitter works on high-pressure pipes filled with liquid or gas, while a sprinkler fitter installs fire sprinkler systems.

Becoming a plumber requires serious study and hard work, but the rewards are many. Not only will you have an opportunity to earn a good wage, but you also will be performing an essential public service.

On the Job

When a residential plumber arrives on a new job, the first task is to analyze what needs to be done and then explain the necessary steps to the client. If there's a leak in a ceiling, for example, a plumber needs to do some detective work to figure out where the leak is located. A plumber then uses plumbing knowledge to decide how to best reach and repair the leak. To reach the source of a leak, a plumber may need to cut into a wall, dig up a floor, or work in a cramped space. In a job at another site, he or she may be called on to replace an outdated kitchen sink or create a plumbing system for a new bathroom. To assemble a system, a plumber often needs to use saws, pipe cutters, and pipe-bending machines to cut and bend lengths of pipe. The pipes then are connected together with adhesives, or soldered together with a torch in the case of copper pipes. Once the work is completed, a plumber tests the plumbing system with pressure gauges to make sure everything is working properly.

Specialty workers perform other tasks. Pipe fitters and steam fitters keep the large piping systems in power plants, office buildings, factories, and water plants working, while pipe layers install the giant pipes used to created municipal water mains, gas lines, drains, and sewers.

No matter the specialty, workers in the plumbing field need to be strong enough to lift heavy materials and have the dexterity to work in awkward conditions both indoors and out. They also need to know how to read blueprints, perform mathematics, and solve problems creatively, and must enjoy working with their hands.

Keys to Success

To be a successful plumber, you need
- solid mathematical skills
- ability to read blueprints
- physical strength
- stamina
- good communication skills
- ability to work with hands

Do You Have What It Takes?

You need the strength to lift heavy pipes, the stamina to work in cramped spaces, and the creativity to design a plumbing system. You also should be good at solving math problems, reading blueprints, creating mechanical drawings, and working with your hands. Good communication skills are helpful as well, because plumbers often need to explain their work to customers.

A Typical Day at Work

A plumber's job varies greatly, depending on the type of work he or she chooses to do. Some plumbers work in a specific location for one company, while others work at various sites throughout the day. Many plumbers work for themselves, so they must be able to judge how long each job will take and how much it will cost.

At the start of a work day, most plumbers look over their scheduled assignments. Depending on the work that needs to be done, a plumber may need to pick up supplies before heading out for the first assignment. At one house, a residential plumber may need to unclog a drain. At another home, he or she may need to put in a plumbing system for a new bathroom. A highly skilled plumber may even be called upon to help design a construction project.

A plumber's work day often starts at 8 or 9 a.m. and wraps up by 5 p.m. or so. However, because plumbing problems can happen at any time, a plumber may sometimes need to make an emergency call after hours or on the weekends. A plumber working on a construction project also may be asked to put in extra hours to meet a pressing deadline.

How to Break In

The best way to become a plumber is to work as an apprentice under the supervision of a skilled plumber. Not only will you gain hands-on experience, but you'll be paid for the work you do.

If you are enrolled in a plumbing program at a community college or trade school, your school will probably be able to help you find an apprenticeship program.

You also can check with local unions, companies, contractors, and other organizations that sponsor apprenticeships. A few to try include the United Association of Journeymen and Apprentices of the Plumbing and Pipefitting Industry (http://www.ua.org/), local employers of the Mechanical Contractors Association of America (http://www.mcaa.org/), and the National Association of Plumbing-Heating-Cooling Contractors (http://www.phccweb.org/).

Expect to spend four to five years working as an apprentice. When you complete your apprenticeship, you'll be recognized as a journeyman who has acquired highly regarded, in-demand plumbing skills.

> **"People usually don't think about plumbing until something goes wrong. People just think it's magic: You flush the toilet and there it goes."**
> —Kat Jowell, plumbing-business co-owner

Two-Year Training

Many community colleges and technical schools offer two-year associate's degree programs that provide the classroom instruction needed to become a skilled plumber. Some schools also offer online associate's degree programs through the National Joint Apprenticeship and Training Committee (http://www.njatc.org).

Many of the subjects you study in school will apply directly to the trade you're learning. For example, when you study physics, you will gain knowledge that will help you safely deal with the liquids and gases used in plumbing. When you study math, you'll learn skills that will help you learn how to measure and install piping systems.

While attending school, a plumbing student typically enters into an apprenticeship program, in which the student is supervised and taught by a licensed plumber.

Apprenticeships generally provide four to five years of on-the-job training plus more than 140 hours of instruction in related subjects, such as drafting, blueprint reading, mathematics, applied physics, chemistry, and safety.

As an apprentice, you'll learn how to identify pipes, use plumbing tools, and safely unload materials. As you become more skilled, you'll learn how to install pipes, put in plumbing fixtures, and eventually design and layout plumbing systems. In many communities, to become a licensed plumber you'll also have to pass an examination that shows you understand the basics of plumbing and know local plumbing codes.

What to Look For in a School

When considering a two-year school, be sure to ask these questions:

☞ Does the school offer related coursework, such as mechanical drawing and plumbing theory?

☞ Does the school provide the latest information on local plumbing codes?

☞ Does the school provide the needed connections to land an apprenticeship?

☞ What is the school's job placement rate?

☞ What are the instructors' credentials? Have they worked in the industry?

☞ Does the school offer the tools needed for hands-on learning?

☞ Does the school offer management, finance, and other business classes for students who eventually want to start their own business?

The Future

The role of a plumber is crucial in today's modern society: Without clean water and sanitary waste facilities, communities would face serious health problems.

Plumbers are needed to repair, maintain, and upgrade existing plumbing systems in private homes and commercial buildings. They also help design plumbing systems in new buildings and work with building contractors to make sure local plumbing ordinances are followed.

Because plumbers provide essential services, and the demand for their skills outstrips the supply of trained plumbers, the plumbing profession probably will continue to be one of the best-paying fields in construction.

Interview with a Professional:
Q&A

Kat Jowell

Co-owner, Aloha Plumbing, North Glenn, Colorado

Q: *How did you get started?*

A: Basically, I am a plumber by marriage. I've been married to my husband for 26 years and I've learned everything I know from him. He started his career in the U.S. Air Force.

Once he got his master's license, we started our own business and I started working for him full time. Basically, I was always his assistant and helper until I obtained enough experience to actually plumb myself.

Q: *What's a typical day like?*

A: We start out early in the morning, calling and confirming all our appointments with our clients. Then we head out. We have a material list that we call into our suppliers for the day's work. We take that and start off for the first job. While we're both working, I have my cell phone and take all the calls that come in.

We do many things at once: We perform the work and manage the office end of it from the field while we're working. We can usually do from four to eight jobs a day. We keep really busy. Usually, on good days, we start at 9 a.m. and work until 5 or 6 p.m.

With plumbing, you never know what you'll run into.

Q: *What's your advice for those starting a career?*

A: Community colleges and trade schools are great for getting into plumbing. It's really good if you're in an apprentice training program. You go to college part time and work for a plumbing company part time. You get hands-on practical experience: There's nothing better when you're learning to become a plumber. Lots of plumbing companies are eager to hire students in apprenticeships.

Q: *What's the best part of being a plumber?*

A: Never having to hire a plumber. That can be expensive.

Seriously, in my case, it's being able to be my own boss. Particularly in my case, it's working with my husband because we're best friends. We make a really great team.

Job Seeking Tips

See the suggestions below and turn to Appendix A for advice on creating a résumé, interviewing for schools or jobs, and collecting references.

✔ Build a portfolio that shows off your various skills.

✔ Decide what you're interested in and seek relevant experience.

✔ Seek advice from the career placement office.

✔ Reach out, and when possible, join associations in your chosen field.

Career Connections

For more information on careers for plumbers, contact the following organizations.

The United Association of Journeymen and Apprentices of the Plumbing and Pipefitting Industry http://www.ua.org

Mechanical Contractors Association of America http://www.mcaa.org

National Association of Plumbing-Heating-Cooling Contractors http://www.phccweb.org

National Center for Construction Education and Research http://www.nccer.org

Associated Builders and Contractors Workforce Development Department http://www.trytools.org

Did You Know?

"It's me, MARIO!" Nintendo's mustachioed character may very well be the world's best-known plumber. Only instead of repairing plumbing fixtures, this video game plumber routinely races through tunnels, jumps over pipes, and escapes from surprise traps.

Associate's Degree Programs

Here are a few schools with two-year plumbing programs:

Maysville Community and Technical College, Maysville, Kentucky

Minnesota State and Community College, Moorhead, Minnesota

Southern Maine Community College, South Portland, Maine

Luzerne County Community College, Nanticoke, Pennsylvania

Central Georgia Technical College, Macon, Georgia

Financial Aid

Here are a few plumbing-related scholarships. For more on financial aid for two-year students, turn to Appendix B.

American Standard Scholarship This scholarship is offered through the Plumbing-Heating-Cooling Contractors Association to students enrolled in an approved apprenticeship program, college, or trade school. http://www.foundation.phccweb.org/Scholarships

Delta Faucet Scholarship This scholarship is for plumbing students enrolled in approved apprenticeships and educational programs. http://www.foundation.phccweb.org/Scholarships/DScholarship.htm

Bradford White Corporation Scholarship Scholarships go to students who are enrolled in an approved apprenticeship program and an accredited two-year community college, technical college, or trade school. http://www.foundation.phccweb.org/Scholarships/BWScholarship.htm

Related Careers

Boilermakers; boiler operators; heating, air-conditioning, and refrigeration mechanics; sheet metal workers; and stationary engineers.

Electrician

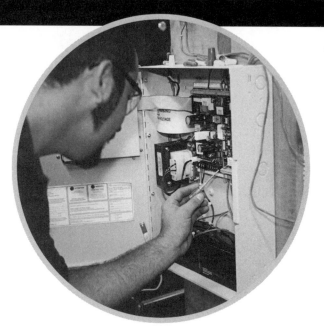

Vital Statistics

Salary: The median earnings are about $20 per hour, or about $41,000 a year (depending on the availability of work), according to the 2006 data from U.S. Bureau of Labor Statistics.

Employment: Growth in the number of electricians is forecast to keep pace with the average for all occupations through 2014, according to the Bureau of Labor Statistics. Professionals are finding increasing opportunities in the computer, telecommunications, and manufacturing industries.

Education: An associate's degree in electrical technology can be completed in as little as 18 months. A good associate's degree program will provide instruction in the principles of electronics and electrical systems, wiring, power transmission, safety, industrial and household appliances, job estimation, electrical testing and inspection, and applicable codes and standards. An associate's degree program may be combined with an apprenticeship lasting three to five years.

Work Environment: An electrician may work indoors or outdoors, depending on the nature of the job.

When you think about a career as an electrician, you probably have some idea already that these professionals install and fix electrical wiring and systems—from air-conditioning to lighting to communication systems. It's great work for someone who likes to solve problems, use some math, and do hands-on work. What you may not realize is that this career is in big demand. The National Association of Electrical Contractors (http://www.necanet.org/) is desperately seeking new electricians. In fact, the electrical industry employs more than 650,000 workers and produces over $65 billion annually. Even as a student learning the trade, you can get right to work and earn up to $37,000 a year, or a total of $50,000 to $75,000 in wages and benefits over the course of an apprenticeship.

As specialists who provide power to the world, electricians work on a wide range of projects. They can work inside, rewiring a remodeled old home that needs to replace decaying wires and update its electrical system. They can work outdoors as a new mall is being constructed, putting in all the electrical fixtures and figuring out the lighting both indoors and in the parking lot. The rapid growth of computers and telecommunications has led to more opportunities for electricians. Also, as factories that produce cars, cell phones, and other products have become more automated, they require the expertise of electricians to maintain and build robotics and sophisticated machinery. It is a career that is in very high demand, and the opportunities are plentiful, especially in areas experiencing a lot of construction growth. Areas of specialization include communications, fire alarm systems, and cranes and elevators.

Electricians have to be fluent at reading *blueprints*. These are basically detailed maps of circuits, outlets, load centers, panel boards, and other equipment. These maps show where current electricity is installed and where it is currently located for repairs. Blueprints may show where conduit (pipe or tubing) is inside partitions, walls, or other concealed areas, or where electrical switches and outlets should be fastened on walls. Often, electricians spend time pulling insulated wires or cables through the tubing to complete circuits between electrical boxes.

On the Job

Being an electrician is very physical. Running wires to refurbish a home or fixing a transformer or generator requires physical endurance and a lot of dexterity and hands-on work. Jobs often demand climbing up scaffolds and ladders or toiling in cramped, dirty, hot, wet, or even very cold conditions. The professionals spend a lot of time joining wires and boxes with specially designed connectors.

Electricity is a very dangerous medium to work with, and these tradespeople must follow very strict regulations. Special testing equipment, such as oscilloscopes, ohmmeters, and voltmeters, test the flow of electricity and make sure circuits are operating correctly. Electricians also use a lot of basic hand tools—screwdrivers, hammers, pliers, hacksaws, and wirestrippers.

Beginners drill holes, set anchors, and set up conduit. As they progress, they measure, fabricate, and install conduit, as well as install, connect, and test wiring, outlets, and switches. They also learn to set up and draw diagrams for entire electrical systems.

Keys to Success

To be a successful electrician, you should have strong
- physical stamina
- manual dexterity
- mathematics skills
- problem-solving ability
- attention to detail

Do You Have What It Takes?

Students who are interested in a career as an electrician should excel at and enjoy courses in mathematics, electronics, mechanical drawing, science, and shop. The job requires that you're in good health and have plenty of stamina and dexterity. Good color vision is essential because workers must identify electrical wires by color.

A Typical Day at Work

Jobs vary widely according to each project, but every electrician has to assess what work needs to be done for the day and how long an entire project with take to complete. Many electricians work for themselves; so they have to be good at estimating how long a job will take and how much it will cost.

A typical day begins by looking over blueprints and determining what can be accomplished in that day. After a long day of manual labor, electricians have to make sure everything is safe and secure as they close down for the night, before resuming work the next day. Most electricians work a 40-hour week, although if the job has a tight deadline, they put in overtime. Electricians who take care of maintenance typically work nights or weekends, and they may be on call and have to work on short notice if there's an emergency. Maintenance electricians also may have periodic extended overtime during scheduled maintenance or retooling periods.

How to Break In

Apprenticeships often lead to employment for budding electricians. They not only provide an opportunity to build skills, but they also offer an opportunity to show that you can be a valuable addition to a company. Apprenticeships often are sponsored by chapters of local unions, such as the International Brotherhood of Electrical Workers, the National Electrical Contractors Association, and the Associated Builders and Contractors and the Independent Electrical Contractors Association.

Electrical apprentices eventually specialize in one of four specialty areas:

- **Outside linemen** install the distribution and transmission lines that move power from power plant to factories, businesses, and homes.
- **Inside wiremen** install power, lighting controls, and other electrical equipment in commercial and industrial buildings.
- **VDV installer technicians** install circuits and equipment for telephones, computer networks, video distribution systems, security and access control systems, and other low-voltage systems.
- **Residential wiremen** install all of the electrical systems in single-family and multifamily houses or dwellings.

Apprentices are paired with journey mentors who help them learn the hands-on skills on actual job sites. Apprentices also may develop contacts for future jobs.

Two-Year Training

Many community colleges and technical schools offer two-year associate's degree programs to become an electrical technician. With an associate's degree, a graduate can work as an electrician in industrial machine installation and repair, electrical/electronic equipment repair, mechanical control and valve repair, programmable controller installation and repair, electrical/electronic equipment assembly, electromechanical systems repair, and automatic machinery maintenance.

Typically, those starting in the field need to combine classroom work with hands-on experience in the form of an apprenticeship. Those in associate's degree programs may have to add on a few years to finish apprenticeship training in order to gain a thorough knowledge of all aspects of the trade. A standard program might take 144 hours of classroom time combined with 2,000 hours of on-the-job training. Once they have successfully completed apprenticeship training, professionals officially become *journeymen.*

Through the American Council on Education (http://www.acenet.edu), apprentices can make sure that their apprenticeship courses are linked to an associate's degree program at a two-year college or technical school. They can also enroll in an online associate's degree program offered by the National Joint Apprenticeship and Training Committee (http://www.njatc.org). Keep in mind too that if you don't want to pursue an associate's degree, you can still enter an apprenticeship program with just a high school diploma.

What to Look For in a School

When considering a two-year school, be sure to ask these questions:

☞ Will the school train me to pass a standard examination on electrical theory, the National Electrical Code, and local electric and building codes?

☞ Will this degree program provide both course work and the connection to an apprenticeship?

☞ What is the school's job placement rate?

☞ What areas of specialization does the school offer in terms of careers as an electrician? For example, robotics, telecommunications, or computers.

☞ What are the professors' credentials? Have they worked in the industry? How available are professors outside of the classroom?

Interview with a Professional:
Q&A

Devlin Gebert

Apprentice electrician, IBEW (International
Brotherhood of Electrical Workers) Local Union #5,
Pittsburgh, Pennsylvania

Q: *How did you get started?*

A: I was interested in becoming an electrician because I love working with
my hands and had an interest in learning something new. I looked into
trade schools and found the electrician's local union had the best to offer.
The local union not only provided me with hands-on training and dedicated classroom attention, but an opportunity to earn an associate's degree
at no cost. After submitting an application, a test similar to the SATs was ad-
ministered. An interview finished off the hiring process.

Q: *What's a typical day like?*

A: My typical day at work starts at 6 a.m. At starting time, hard hats come
on and tools come out. Power tools and building materials are taken to a
designated work area determined by the foreman. Different tasks are as-
signed by the foreman, so you could be doing the same thing for a stretch
of days or a variety of tasks in one day. My job all depends on timing and
coordination with the other trades. Every trade has steps to take to complete the entire project, but there is a logical order that dictates what can be
done and when. An eight-hour day is standard with a 15-minute coffee
break at 9:30 and a half hour lunch at noon. Quitting time is 2:30.

Right now I am installing the underground feeds for a new television
station. The fiberoptic cable requires a four-inch pipe and the power requires a five-inch pipe to be encased in concrete and buried underground.
Each morning an operator excavates the dirt in order for us to set racks, install the pipe, and prepare for concrete. The next day the dirt is backfilled
and we move on down the line.

The previous job was for a university. An old office building was gutted
and new offices were being installed. I pulled wire to feed receptacles,
lights, and fire alarms. Once the drywall was finished and the ceilings were
built, the receptacles, switches, and light fixtures were installed.

Q: *What's your advice for those starting a career?*

A: My advice for someone interested in this field is to contact the local International Brotherhood of Electrical Workers and inquire about the application process and career opportunities.

Q: *What's the best part of being an electrician?*

A: I love this career choice because nothing is the same. The type of environment, job requirements, and people are always changing. You can work in an office, a power plant, a renovated building, or get involved from the ground up on a new building. These changing situations open up opportunities to learn a variety of techniques and new technology. The best part is seeing how everyone's hard work and contributions make projects come together.

The Future

As technology continues to get more sophisticated in the 21st century, opportunities are booming for electricians, especially in the areas of robotics, computers, and telecommunications. The continuing expansion of construction in the United States also should increase the demand for electricians, and as more homeowners update their older homes, they will need electricians to bring their wiring up to code.

Did You Know?

Elvis Presley and George Harrison of the Beatles both started out as electricians. Mike Berlin, the head cinematographer on *Everybody Loves Raymond,* started as an electrician on the set of *The Munsters.*

Job Seeking Tips

See the suggestions below and turn to Appendix A for tips on creating a résumé, interviewing for schools or jobs, and collecting references.

✔ Build a portfolio that shows a range of your styles and talents.

✔ Decide what you're interested in and seek relevant experience.

✔ Talk to the career placement office.

Career Connections

For further information on careers for electricians, contact the following organizations.

National Electrical Contractors Association http://www.necanet.org

International Brotherhood of Electrical Workers http://www.ibew.org

Associate's Degree Programs

Here are a few schools offering quality electrical technician programs:

Tidewater Community College, Portsmouth, Virginia

Bishop State Community College, Mobile, Alabama

Lakeland Community College, Kirtland, Ohio

New England Institute of Technology, Warwick, Rhode Island

"Fortunately, I've also been an electrician, and that's a happy memory for me."
— James MacArthur, actor

Financial Aid

Here are a few electrician-related scholarships. For more on financial aid for two-year students, turn to Appendix B.

IBEW/NECA Electrician Scholarship for Women. This scholarship is intended for women pursuing a career as an electrician or telecommunications installer.   http://www.ibew.org

Kendall Electric, Inc. Scholarship. Recipients shall be enrolled for a minimum of six credits in the Electrical Technology program and maintain a minimum 3.0 GPA. This scholarship requires department recommendation.   http://www.lcc.edu/scholarships/foundation/tc.htm

Related Careers

Electrical apprentice; construction electrician; maintenance electrician; electrical troubleshooter; electrical contractor; technical sales representative; linesman; field service technician; electrical engineering technician; electrical design technician; heating, air-conditioning, and refrigeration mechanic and installer; line installer and repairer; electrical and electronics installer and repairer; electronic home entertainment equipment installer and repairer; and elevator installer and repairer.

Aircraft Mechanic

Vital Statistics

Salary: The median salary for aircraft mechanics and service technicians is $21.77 an hour, or more than $45,000 a year, according to the 2006 data from the U.S. Bureau of Labor Statistics..

Employment: The job outlook is bright for skilled aircraft mechanics working for small commuter and regional airlines. Jobs at the best-paying airlines tend to be very competitive. Growth for the field through 2014 is forecast to be as fast as the average for all occupations, according to the Bureau of Labor Statistics.

Education: About 200 schools in the United States are certified by the Federal Aviation Administration (FAA) to teach aircraft mechanics. While in school, students gain the skills and experience they need to become certified aircraft mechanics. Depending on the desired certification, the initial training can take 18 to 30 months.

Work Environment: Aircraft mechanics usually work in hangars or other indoor spaces. Some aircraft mechanics work outside on the airfield on "flight lines," where they repair aircraft that need emergency repairs.

When a pilot safely lands a plane after a bumpy ride, passengers often applaud his efforts. However, the pilot isn't the only one who deserves recognition for helping a plane land safely. Credit also should go to the aircraft mechanics. These essential workers check engines, landing gear, and other aircraft parts to make sure everything is in working order. When they spot a problem, it's their job to make the needed repairs, often under a tight deadline, so that airlines can keep their flights coming and going on time.

Because of the complexity of aircraft today, some mechanics specialize. Airframe mechanics, for example, are certified to work on any part of an aircraft except the instruments, power plants, and propellers. Power plant mechanics are trained to work on engines and propellers. Combination airframe and power plant mechanics, or A&P employees, work on every part of a plane except its instruments. Avionic technicians take care of a plane's weather radar systems, flight instruments, and radio communications.

To become aircraft mechanics, students typically attend an FAA-approved school, where they learn how to inspect, service, repair, and overhaul all kinds of aircraft.

Of the 142,000 people who work as aircraft and avionics equipment mechanics and service technicians, about half work for air transportation companies. Others work for the U.S. government, companies that make aircraft and parts, and firms that own their own planes.

The type of work an aircraft mechanic does often determines where she or he lives. Aircraft mechanics who work at major airports, for example, often live near big cities. Because aerospace manufacturing firms usually are located in California and Washington State, mechanics who work for those firms live on the west coast. Some mechanics work directly for the FAA, which has facilities in several cities, including Oklahoma City, Okla., Atlantic City, N.J., Wichita, Kans., and Washington, D.C.

Aircraft mechanics are well paid, with the highest wages going to experienced workers who are qualified to perform multiple tasks. The average median income tops $45,000 a year, with high earners making more than $70,000 a year. As an added bonus, workers at major airlines often receive generous travel discounts.

Being an aircraft mechanic is a demanding job that can't be taken lightly. No matter the pressure, aircraft mechanics can't afford to cut corners to speed up the job. Their careful attention to detail helps keeps air travelers safe.

On the Job

Aircraft mechanics service, repair, overhaul, and test aircraft. To do all these tasks, a mechanic has to be fit enough to climb up on scaffolds and ladders, crawl under wings, fit into tight spaces, and lift parts that can weigh 50 pounds.

Inspecting aircraft requires a mechanic to pay attention to the details. She or he must carefully examine and inspect engines and other aircraft equipment for cracks, breaks, and leaks. While working, the mechanic uses various hand tools, gauges, and equipment to adjust, align, and calibrate aircraft systems.

Communication skills are crucial because mechanics have to read and understand complex technical manuals and write clearly written detailed reports. Speed and attention to detail also are vital skills: When a pilot discovers a problem during a preflight test, mechanics working on the airfield must quickly diagnose the problem and make any needed repairs. The pressure can be intense. But no matter how much an airline wants the planes to fly on time, mechanics can't cut corners to speed up a job.

Keys to Success

To be successful as an aircraft mechanic, you must be or have
- detail-oriented
- mechanical aptitude
- troubleshooter
- able to handle stress
- physical strength and agility

- a problem solver
- strong math skills

Do You Have What It Takes?

To be an aircraft mechanic, you need a mechanical aptitude, strong computing skills, and a solid understanding of electronics. You need to be a good troubleshooter, a careful and thorough worker, and be physically fit. You must be able to work under pressure in a job that requires you to maintain safety standards while helping an airline stick to its flight schedules. You need to be agile enough to work on all sorts of aircraft. Because aircraft mechanics sometimes need to work on top of wings and fuselages of large planes, the job isn't suitable for someone who is afraid of heights.

A Typical Day at Work

Aircraft mechanics work eight-hour shifts around the clock with frequent opportunities for overtime work. They conduct routine inspections on aircraft. To examine an engine, a mechanic may remove it from the plane with a lift, or reach it from a ladder or scaffold.

With the help of special instruments, mechanics check parts for wear. They use X-rays and magnetic inspection equipment to look for invisible cracks. If they find a problem, they repair the part or replace it with a new one. Once all the repairs are made, they test the new equipment to make sure it is working properly.

When a pilot notices a problem or detects a faulty piece of equipment during a preflight check, he'll often share the information with a mechanic, who will then work quickly to make the needed fixes, so the plane can take off safely.

How to Break In

Attending an FAA-certified school can help you get the training and certification you need to be an aircraft mechanic. You can view a list of certified schools at http://av-info.faa.gov/MaintenanceSchool.asp. While receiving training, aircraft mechanics are required to work under the supervision of a certified mechanic. After 18 months of experience in either airframe or power plant work, or a combination of 30 months in both, a worker can take an FAA certification examination.

A worker who passes the examination can work on her or his own.

Those just starting out usually work at smaller airlines. As mechanics gain experience, sometimes they become lead mechanic, crew chief, inspector, or shop supervisor.

The best-paying jobs tend to go to those with the most experience and those who have cross-trained and are certified to work in more than one area. Because aircraft technology is constantly changing, workers must continually work to keep their skills up to date.

Aircraft mechanics are required to have their own hand tools, which are expensive. To ease the costs, schools often lend tools to students and some employers offer payment plans to help beginners buy what they need.

Two-Year Training

Students taking courses in airframe mechanics learn about sheet metal structures, ice and rain control systems, hydraulics, fuel systems, and other topics. Those taking power plant courses learn how to inspect and work on engines, power plant lubrication systems, propellers, and ignition systems.

Only certified mechanics can work without supervision. For example, students with 18 months of experience in airframe or power plant work can take an FAA certification examination. Workers who pass the examination then are certified to work on their own.

Students also may find it helpful to take classes in math, physics, chemistry, electronics, computer science, and mechanical drawing because many of these subjects' principles apply to the operation and maintenance of aircraft.

What to Look For in a School

When considering a two-year school, be sure to ask these questions:

☞ Is the school certified by the FAA?

☞ Does the school have a job placement office? What is its job placement rate? How good are the jobs that students land?

☞ Does the program prepare students to take the required certification examinations? What percentage of students pass the examinations?

☞ What are the instructors' credentials? Have they worked in the industry? Have they kept up with new techniques and procedures? Are they available outside the classroom?

☞ Do the classrooms and labs have up-to-date equipment?

Did You Know?

In 1938, Douglas "Wrong Way" Corrigan got "lost" flying from New York to California and ended up in Ireland. But did he really get lost? Corrrigan, who was also a skilled aircraft mechanic, had recently modified his plane so it could fly across the Atlantic, so many people think he knew exactly where he was headed.

Interview with a Professional:
Q&A

Ed Martinkus
Director of maintenance, DB Aviation, Waukegan, Illinois

Q: *How did you get started?*

A: I grew up right next to Midway airport, so I always had airplanes either landing or taking off, and going over the house as a kid. I was always mechanically inclined. When I got out of high school, the counselor suggested I do aircraft mechanics instead of auto mechanics.

Q: *What's a typical day like?*

A: Being a mechanic, you handle day-to-day problems with aircraft. You do post-flight inspections after the aircraft gets back. You do routine maintenance, liking changing tires and light bulbs. When you see the same airplane all the time, you are constantly looking for little things that may lead to large things. You're looking to head off problems.

Q: *What's your advice for those starting a career?*

A: Aircraft mechanics is totally different than when I got into it. If you don't have any computer skills, you can't do this job. Be involved in your career. That was my main thing. I joined PAMA (Professional Aviation Maintenance Association) right away when I got out of school. When you join an organization, get involved in the activities. If you network yourself really well, you can do well. If you lose a job or you want to look for another job, it's a lot easier if you network and you know all the players.

Q: *What's the best part about being an aircraft mechanic?*

A: The gratification of getting the aircraft repaired and seeing it fly is a very cool thing.

Job Seeking Tips

See the suggestions below and look in Appendix A for advice on creating a résumé, interviewing for schools or jobs, and collecting references.

✔ Train and earn certificates in different areas to show off your versatility as an employee.

✔ Decide what you're interested in and seek relevant experience.

✔ Seek advice from the career placement office.

✔ Reach out to associations in your chosen field.

The Future

Job opportunities are expected to be the greatest at small commuter and regional airlines, and in general aviation. Large airlines pay better wages but
competition for those jobs can be fierce. Aircraft mechanics can make
themselves more valuable by becoming specialists in more than one area.

> **"The aircraft comes in. The aircraft mechanic goes out
> there and fixes it. The plane takes off and flies. That's
> all aircraft mechanics need. They don't need 11 World
> War II movies made about aircraft mechanics like pi-
> lots do. They don't need the glory. They don't need a
> pat on the back. They just want to do a good job."**
> —Ed Martinkus, aircraft-maintenance director

Career Connections

For more information on careers for aircraft, contact the following organizations.

Professional Aviation Maintenance Association http://www.pama.org

USAJOBS http://www.usajobs.opm.gov

FAA listing of maintenance schools http://av-info.faa.gov/
maintenanceschool.asp

Association for Women in Aviation Maintenance http://www
.awam.org

Federal Aviation Administration http://www.faa.gov

International Association of Machinists and Aerospace Workers
http://www.iamaw.org

Associate's Degree Programs

Here are a few schools offering quality aircraft mechanic programs:

Michigan Institute of Aviation and Technology, Belleville, Michigan

National Aviation Academy, Clearwater, Florida

Spartan College of Aeronautics and Technology, Tulsa, Oklahoma

Stratford School for Aviation Maintenance Technicians, Stratford, Connecticut

Glendale, Community College District, Glendale, California

Financial Aid

Here are some scholarships for those pursuing an education as an aircraft mechanic. Appendix B provides tips and other financial aid resources for two-year students.

PAMA Foundation Scholarship Program awards scholarships to students studying aviation mechanics.   http://www.pama.org

The Bud Grover Memorial Scholarship goes to students enrolled in an accredited school in an avionics or aircraft repair program. http://www.aea.net/EducationalFoundation

David Arver Memorial Scholarship goes to high school seniors and/or college students who plan to or are attending an accredited school in an avionics or aircraft repair program. http://www.aea.net/EducationalFoundation

Pacific Southwest Instruments awards the Lee Tarbox Memorial Scholarship to students in an accredited school in avionics or aircraft repair program.   http://www.aea.net/EducationalFoundation

Experimental Aircraft Association provides scholarships for students enrolled in aviation programs.   http://www.youngeagles.com/ programs/scholarships

Related Careers

Automobile mechanic, bus and truck mechanic, diesel engine specialist, electrician, electrical and electronic installer, electrical and electronic repairer.

Auto Service Technician

Vital Statistics

Salary: The median hourly wage for automobile service technicians and mechanics is $15.60 an hour, or about $32,450 a year, according to 2006 data from the U.S. Bureau of Labor Statistics. Top earners can make more than $54,500 a year.

Employment: The demand for skilled auto service technicians and mechanics is good—especially for those who can diagnose complex problems, work with computers, and understand electronics. Growth in the field is forecast to be as fast as the average for all occupations through 2014, according to the Bureau of Labor Statistics.

Education: A two-year associate's degree program in automobile technology provides a solid grounding for students in this field. Many auto manufacturers and dealers have partnerships with schools that give students a chance to work in service departments under the watchful eyes of skilled technicians.

Work Environment: Service technicians usually work inside repair shops.

Love a good mystery? As an auto service technician, you'll have plenty of chances to solve puzzling mysteries while working on a wide variety of cars from convertibles to sports cars to family station wagons. When a customer brings in a car for repair, an auto technician's task is to diagnose and solve the problem. To collect clues, he or she asks the customer to describe the car's symptoms. Using knowledge of auto mechanics, computer systems, and electronics, he or she then considers the likely suspects. Depending on the problem, the technician may need to take the vehicle for a test drive or put it through some diagnostic tests. If all goes well, the technician will be able to quickly diagnose the problem and make any needed repairs.

Being able to solve such automotive mysteries takes practice and training, both in school and on the job. In fact, because cars often require high-tech expertise, workers in the auto service industry today are commonly referred to as technicians instead of mechanics. Not only do today's workers need to work with hand tools, but they must master electronic diagnostic equipment and computer-based technical guides.

To help ensure that there are enough workers with the skills needed to maintain and repair today's increasingly complex cars, manufacturers and auto dealers have partnered with community colleges and trade schools that offer courses in automotive repair. Students enrolled in these programs are given opportunities to work under the supervision of skilled auto technicians in local dealers' service shops.

Because cars are continually changing, an auto service technician's educational training doesn't end once he or she completes a two-year degree. While on the job, many employers offer workers opportunities to attend special training programs through various car makers. In bigger repair shops, some workers specialize in a particular area. Automotive air-conditioning repairers install, service, and fix air conditioners in cars. Tune-up technicians focus on making sure a car's ignition timing, spark plugs, and emissions control system are set for optimal performance. Other specialists include front-end mechanics, brake repairers, transmission technicians, and car body rebuilders.

More than 800,000 people work in the auto service industry today, with the median salary hovering just above $32,000, according to the U.S. Bureau of Labor Statistics. Those working for local governments and automobile dealers tend to earn more, with median salaries topping $38,000 a year. Median salaries for workers in automotive repair and maintenance shops and gasoline stations are about $28,000 a year. Top earners in the industry make more than $54,000 a year. Those who end up running their own business can earn even more.

Employers generally provide the big-ticket items, such as power tools and engine analyzers, but individual workers are expected to have their own hand tools.

On the Job

Being an auto service technician requires mental and physical dexterity. Workers rely on their analytical and diagnostic skills when trying to decide what's wrong with a car. While doing so, they may look at the car's parts, hook it up to a diagnostic program, or even take it for a test drive. By the end of the day, a hard-working technician often will be covered in grease and dirt.

The tools needed to service and repair a car vary greatly, depending on the job. Some problems can be solved with a quick computerized adjustment. Others require technicians to use hand, power, and machine tools. For example, technicians need jacks and hoists to lift cars. They work on exhaust systems with welding and flame-cutting tools. Small tools, such as screwdrivers, pliers, and wrenches, come in handy, when working on tiny parts in hard-to-reach places.

Looking over a car to make sure it's working properly is an important part of a service technician's job. Many technicians follow a checklist—making sure critical parts, such as belts, brakes, and fluid systems are in good shape. The best mechanics will spot worn parts before they cause untimely breakdowns on the road or do severe damage to essential car components.

Auto service technicians often have to explain problems to customers. Having good communication skills, including the ability to translate jargon, helps build good will and repeat business.

Keys to Success

To succeed as an auto service technician, you should have

- mathematical ability
- mechanical aptitude
- solid computer skills
- good communication skills
- attention to detail

Do You Have What It Takes?

To be a successful auto service technician, you need to be a creative problem solver with strong diagnostic skills. You should like cars, enjoy working with your hands, and have a solid background in math, computing, and electronics. If you're obsessed with reading car magazines and interested in working on your own car, this career could be for you. Because car designs are always changing, the savviest workers are always looking for opportunities to update their skills and knowledge. Good communication skills can help you write clear work orders and explain car repairs to customers.

A Typical Day at Work

Gauging the time needed for various repair and service jobs and prioritizing work are crucial parts of the job, especially if you run your own auto repair shop. As the owner or manager of a shop, you want to take in enough work to keep busy and make money; but if you take in more than you—and your workers—can handle, you'll end up with unhappy customers.

Even once the schedule is set, workers often need to readjust their plans. For example, work on one car may need to be postponed until a necessary part arrives. What originally looked like a routine service sometimes can turn into a major repair job.

Auto service technicians often work more than 40 hours each week. Because cars don't always break down between 9 a.m. and 5 p.m. during the week, some technicians also work on nights and weekends.

How to Break In

While still in high school, you can bolster your chances for success by taking courses in electronics, physics, chemistry, English, computers, and mathematics. Some high schools even offer courses in auto mechanics.

Once you're enrolled in a trade school or community college, look for opportunities to receive on-the-job training. Some schools have partnerships with automobile manufacturers and dealers who pay students to work under the supervision of trained mechanics. Not only will you pick up invaluable skills, but if you do a good job, once your training is completed, your employer may offer you a permanent position. Certification programs that show you've mastered a particular skill will make you a more competitive job candidate.

> **"If you're open all day on Saturday, you get all the problem cars that people try to fix themselves on Saturday morning."**
> —Joe Torchiana, tire-service business owner

Two-Year Training

Many community colleges and technical schools offer two-year associate's degree programs for students who want to be auto service technicians. In addition to providing auto service instruction, some schools teach courses in English, basic math, computers, customer service, and communications. Believe it or not, these courses will help you be a better auto technician. For example, the math you learn will help you calculate gear ratios, and the physics you study will help you understand hydraulics in cars.

In automotive technology classes, you'll start with the basics. You'll learn how to work with power tools and perform basic maintenance on cars. Eventually you'll advance to more complex courses, in which you'll learn how to overhaul engines and service electrical systems on cars.

Beginners in the industry usually start as trainee technicians, technician helpers, or lubrication workers. As they gain more skills and education, workers are given a chance to perform basic service tasks and simple repairs. It usually takes two to five years of on-the-job experience to become a journeyman-level service technician. Complex specialties, such as transmission repair, typically require an additional year or two of training.

Receiving certification from the National Institute for Automotive Service Excellence (ASE) in eight specific areas, such as electrical systems, engine repair, and brake repair, can help an auto service technician establish credentials. To qualify, you need to pass an examination and have two years of experience, or if you have completed automotive training in a school, you need just one year of experience. To be certified as a master automobile technician, you need to be certified in all eight areas.

What to Look For in a School

When considering a two-year school, be sure to ask these questions:

☞ Does the school have a partnership with a manufacturer, dealer, or other firm that provides on-the-job training?

☞ What are the instructors' credentials? Have they worked in the industry? Do they have contacts in the industry? Are they available outside of the classroom?

☞ Has the curriculum kept up with changes in the industry? Will you have a chance to work on late-model vehicles?

☞ What is the school's job placement rate?

☞ What areas of specialization does the school offer; for example, automotive air-conditioning, transmissions, or front-end mechanisms?

☞ Is the school approved by the Accrediting Commission of Career Schools and Colleges of Technology (http://www.accsct.org)?

The Future

As cars continue to become more complex, and thus more difficult to repair, auto service technicians with training in electronics and computers will continue to be in high demand.

The bulk of job growth in this field will come from service centers in automobile dealerships and independent repair shops. Retail operations that focus on specific tasks, such as oil changes and air conditioning services, also will create new jobs. With the growth of self-serve stations, the opportunities for repair work in traditional service stations will probably decline.

Did You Know?

When comedian Jay Leno isn't cracking jokes, he's often working on a vehicle in his prized collection of cars, or penning a "Garage" column for *Popular Mechanics* magazine.

Job Seeking Tips

See the suggestions below and look in Appendix A for advice on creating a résumé, interviewing for schools or jobs, and collecting references.

✔ Work to become certified in several specialties of auto repair.

✔ Decide what you're interested in and seek relevant experience.

✔ Reach out to relevant organizations, such as the Automotive Youth Educational Systems, the National Automotive Technicians Education Foundation, and the National Automobile Dealers Association.

✔ Check with your school to see if they have partnerships with local dealers who provide on-the-job training to qualified students.

✔ Talk to the career placement office.

Interview with a Professional:
Q&A
Joe Torchiana
Owner, One Stop Tire and Auto, West Chester, Pennsylvania

Q: *How did you get started?*

A: I started in automotive repair when I was 15. The last stop on my paper route was a Sunoco Service Station. I would leave the paper there, and just hang around, watching the guys, seeing what was going on. When I turned 15, they offered me a job.

In college, I earned a full electrical engineering degree, but I didn't really want to do it at the time. So when I got out of Villanova, I went to work as a service technician at a Volkswagen dealership. About 18 years ago, we built the facility where we are now and we've lived happily ever after.

Q: *What's a typical day like?*

A: The day starts at 7:30 a.m. I'm greeting customers, finding out what their concerns are, and making up work orders. I'm in the trenches all day. We work till 6 p.m. five days a week. By the time Friday rolls around, we've put in 55 hours.

Q: *What's your advice for those starting a career?*

A: Get all the education that you can. Know going in that you're going to have to continue your education in the magnitude of 100 to 150 hours a year. Get as many certifications as you can, and as early, as you can.

Q: *What's the best part of being an auto service technician?*

A: The best part is being able to diagnose something and fix it.

Career Connections

For more information on automotive careers, contact the following organizations.

National Automotive Technicians Education Foundation
http://www.natef.org

Automotive Youth Educational Systems (AYES) http://www.ayes.org

National Institute for Automotive Service Excellence
http://www.asecert.org

National Automobile Dealers Association http://www.nada.org

Automotive Retailing Today http://www.autoretailing.org

Automotive Jobs Today http://www.autojobstoday.org

Career Voyages (U.S. Department of Labor)   http://www.career
voyages.gov/automotive-main.cfm

Associate's Degree Programs

Here are a few schools offering quality auto service technician programs:

Advanced Technology Institute, Virginia Beach, Virginia

IntelliTec College, Grand Junction, Colorado

Western Technical College, El Paso, Texas

WyoTech, Freemont, California

Lincoln Technical Institute, Indianapolis, Indiana

Financial Aid

Here are a few automotive scholarships. For more on financial aid for two-year students, turn to Appendix B.

GM Automotive Service Educational Scholarship Program awards scholarships for further study to graduates of the Automotive Youth Educational Systems Program (AYES).   http://www.ayes.org/students/scholarships

John F. Smith, Jr. (JFS) Scholarship Award helps AYES students continue their studies in an accredited two-year program or an approved educational partnership with an auto maker. http://www.ayes.org/students/scholarships

Jon H. Poteat Scholarships are awarded to students in the National Technical Honor Society.   http://www.nths.org/Student/Scholarships.asp

Related Careers

Automotive body repairer, diesel service technician, diesel service mechanic, and small engine mechanic.

HVACR
Engineering
Technician

Vital Statistics

Salary: The median wage for heating, ventilation, air-conditioning, and refrigeration (HVACR) mechanics and installers is $17.43 an hour, or more than $36,000 a year, according to 2006 data from the U.S. Bureau of Labor Statistics.

Employment: The demand for skilled HVACR engineers is high and is expected to continue to grow. The field is expected to grow as fast as the average for all occupations through 2014, according to the Bureau of Labor Statistics.

Education: Accredited schools and apprenticeships provide essential instruction and training for people who want to work in the heating, ventilation, air-conditioning, and refrigeration industry. Once a student gains the required skills, she or he can take industry examinations, which often lead to better-paying jobs.

Work Environment: Even though technicians often work indoors, work conditions can be uncomfortable. For example, you may have to repair a broken heater during a winter storm or fix an air-conditioning system during a heat wave.

Years ago, when the weather grew unbearably hot, people simply had to suffer through. Life is much easier in today's modern society. On steamy days, we can escape into the air-conditioned comfort of homes, offices, and stores. Likewise, before refrigeration, homemakers had to rely on blocks of ice to keep perishable foods from spoiling. Thanks to modern refrigeration systems, perishable foods today stay fresh longer and once-exotic treats can now be shipped safely from afar.

Not only have such advances in HVACR industry made modern life comfortable, but they also have helped boost the U.S. economy. As you can imagine, the demand for skilled HVACR workers who keep these vital systems running is high. Top earners make more than $56,000 a year and 15 percent of HVACR workers eventually go into business for themselves.

Due the complexity of HVACR systems, workers in this field need to be highly trained and skilled. A two-year degree program that specializes in HVACR-related courses provides a solid background. While in school, you'll learn about the theory and design that go into installing and running heating, ventilation, air-conditioning, and refrigeration systems. You'll also learn important safety rules that will help keep you—and others—protected. HVACR workers also help keep us healthy. For example, when an HVACR worker designs a heating and ventilation system for a new home, he or she programs the system to keep the humidity low, which in turn limits the growth of mold, dust mites, and other microorganisms that can make us ill. When designing a system in an office, a store, or other commercial building, HVACR workers have to meet specific air quality guidelines. They must make sure enough fresh air is being ventilated throughout the building and that the vented air is safe to breathe. Depending on the environment, HVACR designers may need to put in filters to prevent pollen, monoxide, dust, and other pollutants from entering the building.

Schools often help students join apprenticeship programs, in which they receive on-the-job training while earning money. As a beginning apprentice, you'll earn wages that are about half the rate of more experienced workers. As you gain new skills, your pay will usually go up too. One sure route to higher wages—and better jobs—is to take and pass various accreditation examinations in the HVACR industry.

Due to the complexity of HVACR systems, many technicians eventually specialize in one area. Some workers focus on installation, while others concentrate on keeping systems in good repair. Some HVACR workers become experts in refrigeration, while others specialize in heating and/or air-conditioning systems.

Of the more than 270,000 workers in the field, about half work for plumbing, heating, and air-conditioning contractors. Some work directly for air-conditioning and refrigeration services, while others are employed in stores and repair shops. Some work in large buildings that need employees to operate and maintain their air conditioning, ventilation, refrigeration, and heating systems. No matter where they work, HVACR workers make life more comfortable.

On the Job

A blueprint is an HVACR worker's map. Before putting in a new air-conditioning system, an HVACR installer looks over the blueprint to see which parts need to go where. Using the blueprint as a guide, she or he places the system's fuel lines, water lines, air ducts, vents, pumps, and other parts in their proper positions. While piecing a system together, the installer also creates connections for electrical wires and system controls.

HVACR systems are made up of many parts, including motors, compressors, pumps, fans, ducts, pipes, thermostats, and switches. An HVACR technician must understand how each of those parts works and how it relates to the rest of the system.

Keeping HVACR systems up and running, as well as repairing ones that break down, is often done by HVACR workers who specialize in maintenance and repair. Depending on the job, a maintenance worker may need to clean parts, replace filters, cut and connect pipes, and adjust control switches. To make sure furnace and air-conditioning systems are running efficiently, they check for leaks, adjust burners and blowers, and check the thermostat.

While on the job, an HVACR technician uses a variety of tools, such as hammers, pipe cutters, wrenches, and torches. The technician checks electric currents with a voltmeter, measures refrigerant pressure with a pressure gauge, and checks the temperature with a thermometer.

One crucial role air-conditioning and refrigeration technicians play is the safe recovery of harmful refrigerants that are used in refrigeration and air-conditioning systems. These refrigerants can damage the environment, and when technicians work on systems that use these refrigerants, they have to follow strict disposal rules.

Keys to Success

To be a successful HVACR engineering technician, you need

- the ability to read blueprints
- good communication skills
- enough strength to lift heavy equipment
- solid math skills
- a basic understanding of electronics and plumbing
- to be good at fixing things
- to be able to figure out how things work

Do You Have What It Takes?

To work in the HVACR field, you need to be a creative problem solver, detail oriented, good in math, and you must enjoy working with your hands. You also should be a good communicator. While in high school, you can get a head start on your career by taking courses in computer applications, drafting, physics, chemistry, and math. Some high schools even offer basic courses in HVACR.

A Typical Day at Work

Most mechanics and installers work at least 40 hours each week. Those who maintain and repair systems often work overtime and make repairs at night and during the weekends. Some technicians work at a specific place all day, while others, especially those who make service calls, may travel from site to site.

Some assignments, such as installing a new air-conditioning system in an office building, may require a long-term commitment, while other tasks, such as performing routine maintenance on a furnace system in a home, often can be wrapped up in about an hour.

How to Break In

Your school can often help you join an apprenticeship program, in which you'll have a chance to receive on-the-job training while being paid. Local chapters of national organizations, such as the Air Conditioning Contractors of America and the Mechanical Contractors Association of America, also can help set up apprenticeships.

An apprenticeship usually lasts three to five years. During that time, you'll have a chance to work under the supervision of skilled professionals. You'll also take classes in which you'll learn how to read blueprints, use and care for tools, and design the various HVACR systems.

> **"Be honest. Go out there and treat the people like you want them to treat you. It'll come back to you like a tidal wave."**
> —Wayne Carothers, air-conditioning business owner

Two-Year Training

As HVACR systems have become more complicated, so too has the need for specialized training. Enrolling in a two-year program that focuses on HVACR-related classes can help you get started on the right career path. During your studies, you will learn about electronics and the principles of refrigeration. Eventually you will earn how to install and care for HVACR systems in homes and commercial buildings.

Your school usually can help you find an apprenticeship program in which you'll receive on-the-job training.

When you first start working as an apprentice, you'll take on basic tasks. For example, you may be asked to carry equipment to a site, clean out furnaces, or insulate refrigeration lines. As you gain more experience, you'll be able to move on to more demanding tasks, such as checking electrical circuits and soldering pipes.

Because of the complexity of the systems, you'll have to pass various competency examinations before you can perform some tasks on your own. For example, before you can work with various refrigerants, you need to pass a series of examinations that show you can safely handle them. You also must pass examinations before working with certain types of equipment, such as oil-burning furnaces. Workers with the highest levels of certification often end up being the best-paid workers in the field.

What to Look For in a School

When considering a two-year school, be sure to ask these questions:

☞ Does the school offer work-related courses that teach the basics of installation, maintenance, and repair?

☞ Is the school accredited by the National Center for Construction Education and Research (NCCER) (http://www.nccer.org/index.asp), the Partnership for Air Conditioning, Heating and Refrigeration Accreditation (PAHRA) (http://www.pahrahvacr.org/), or HVAC Excellence (http://www.hvacexcellence.org/)?

☞ Does the school have contacts to help students become apprentices?

☞ What is the school's job placement rate?

☞ Will the program prepare you to take and pass the required certification examinations?

☞ What are the instructors' credentials? Have they worked in the industry? Have they kept up with new techniques and procedures in the industry? Are they available outside the classroom?

☞ Do the classrooms and labs have up-to-date equipment?

☞ Does the school offer management, finance, and other business classes for students who hope to go into business for themselves?

The Future

As HVACR systems become increasingly complex, the demand for highly skilled workers will continue to grow. Environmental concerns will create additional opportunities in this field as companies take steps to improve air quality in buildings and replace old refrigerants with more environmentally friendly ones. Concerns about air quality in buildings coupled with a growing demand for refrigerated equipment in stores and gasoline stations that sell food will boost the need for skilled HVACR technicians. In fact, the U.S. Bureau of Labor Statistics projects that jobs in this industry will increase faster than average for all occupations through 2014. Those who pass various accreditation examinations will be especially sought after.

Did You Know?

The introduction of central air-conditioning, or "man-made weather in the 1920s," helped turn Miami, Houston, and other Sunbelt cities into boomtowns.

Interview with a Professional:
Q&A
Wayne Carothers
Owner, Carr Air Conditioning and Heating, Inc.,
Clearwater, Florida

Q: *How did you get started?*

A: When I got out of the army in 1972, I took my father's advice to learn a trade. I checked into the Pinellas Vocational Institute and took an aptitude test. They said, "Why don't you try the HVACR trade?" That's how I got into it.

I used my GE bill and I went there for two years. The school had a co-op program where they got you a job. I had a number of jobs but eventually I took the state exam and went into my own business in June of 1982.

Q: *What's a typical day like?*

A: On an average day I get up at 5:30 a.m. I'm down at the shop by 7. The guys usually get in at 7:30. It's total chaos until 5 or 5:30 p.m. The mornings are always the busiest. I have to get the guys going on the jobs I have planned for them.

I have five trucks. Three are for the installers. One is mine. Another is for service. I do a lot the night before to prepare for the next day. I try to get them all out by 8 a.m.

The phones start to ring constantly about 8 a.m. Most of my customers are residential customers. It's the usual things: The system isn't working. They hear a noise. They have a condensation problem. Mostly, when it gets hot, they know something's wrong.

My service person usually has four or five different stops a day. Sometimes we can fit in an emergency. The installers are usually set up a couple of days before. They come in, load up with the materials they need, and then they head out. I'm their support person. If they need a part or have a problem, they call me.

Q: *What's your advice for those starting a career?*

A: My advice to young people who are trade-oriented is, if you can, start in high school. Learn the trade the old-fashioned way: Become an apprentice. Learn from an experienced HVACR worker. There's a bright future for anyone who wants to go into it. The pay is good. It's a trade that will always be in demand.

(continued on next page)

(continued from previous page)

We need tradespeople. The appliances today are like automobiles, they're becoming more complicated all the time. I love that the trade is constantly changing. New products are always coming out.

Q: *What's the best part of being an HVACR worker?*

A: I love it when the customers call and say, "What a great crew you have!" I'm always quick to share the good news with them. Knowing the job was put in right and the customer is happy is very satisfying.

Job Seeking Tips

See the suggestions below and look in Appendix A for advice on creating a résumé, interviewing for schools or jobs, and collecting references.

✔ Become certified in specific areas of the industry.

✔ Decide what you're interested in and seek relevant experience.

✔ Seek advice from the career placement office.

✔ Reach out to associations in your chosen field.

Career Connections

For more information on HVACR careers, contact the following organizations.

Air Conditioning Contractors of America http://www.acca.org

Refrigeration Service Engineers Society http://www.rses.org

Plumbing-Heating-Cooling Contractors http://www.phccweb.org

Sheet Metal and Air Conditioning Contractors National Association http://www.smacna.org

HVAC Excellence http://www.hvacexcellence.org

National Technical Honor Society http://www.nths.org

Air-Conditioning and Refrigeration Institute http://www.ari.org/

Mechanical Contractors Association of America http://www.mcaa.org

Associate's Degree Programs

Here are a few schools offering quality HVACR programs:

Austin Community College, Austin, Texas

Northeast Wisconsin Technical College, Green Bay, Wisconsin

Pennsylvania College of Technology, Williamsport, Pennsylvania

Hudson Valley Community College, Troy, New York

North Arkansas College, Harrison, Arkansas

Financial Aid

Here are a few HVACR-related scholarships. For more on financial aid for two-year students, turn to Appendix B.

Clifford H. "Ted" Rees Jr. Scholarship is awarded to students who attend or plan to attend an HVACR training program at an accredited school.   http://www.reesscholarship.org

Bradford White Corporation awards scholarships to HVACR or plumbing students enrolled in an accredited school and an approved apprenticeship program.   http://www.foundation.phccweb.org/Scholarships/BWScholarship.htm

American Society of Heating, Refrigerating and Air-Conditioning Engineers awards Associate Degree Engineering Technology Scholarships to students enrolled in approved two-year programs leading to a career in HVACR.   http://www.ashrae.org

Related Careers

Electrician, sheet metal worker, plumber, pipe layer, pipe fitter, steam fitter, and home appliance repairer.

Surveyor

Vital Statistics

Salary: The median annual salary for surveyors is about $43,000, according to 2006 data from the U.S. Bureau of Labor Statistics. The top 10 percent earn more than $71,600 a year. Starting salaries for surveying technicians with a two-year degree average about $25,000 a year, according to the Bureau of Labor Statistics and the National Society of Professional Surveyors.

Employment: The job outlook is good for surveyors who've taken the required college course work, passed certification examinations, and exhibit strong technical skills. The Bureau of Labor Statistics forecasts that through 2014 growth in the field will be about as fast as the average for all occupations.

Education: Community colleges, trade schools, and universities offer programs in surveying and surveying technology. Courses can be completed in as little as one to two years; those who seek advanced training can pursue a bachelor's degree.

Work Environment: Surveyors spend a lot of time outside, where they take measurements and collect data. They also work indoors, planning surveys, preparing reports, making maps, and searching court records for deed information.

Whether you're putting up a fence or simply selling property, knowing exactly where land begins and ends is vital. To determine official boundaries, homeowners, governments, and businesses hire surveyors to accurately measure distances, direction, and angles between points. Depending on the assignment, a surveyor might describe the boundaries in a deed to a home, define the airspace at an airport, or measure a construction site so workers know exactly where to put a new structure.

Surveyors traditionally have done much of their measuring by hand, using chains, transits, plumb lines, and other tools. However, technological advances have changed the way many surveyors do their work. Some now work with Global Positioning Systems (GPS), which receive signals from satellites in space to help workers pinpoint locations on the ground. Surveyors also use other high-tech gear, including laptops, cameras, and electronic distance-measuring tools. When surveyors aren't in the field, they're inside researching property deeds, creating maps, and writing reports.

A two-year program coupled with job experience can help you get a foothold in the industry. Beginners often start out as assistants or technicians. Assistants hold and position the vertical rods used to measure angles, distances, and elevations. They also compile notes, make sketches, and enter data into computers. Mapping technicians work with field notes to create and check maps for accuracy.

Most states require that surveyors meet specific licensing requirements. In addition, the National Society of Professional Surveyors offers certification to candidates who meet its testing and training requirements. While not mandatory, gaining certification helps establish you as a serious job candidate in this field.

Surveyors generally are well paid, with the median annual salary averaging about $43,000. The median annual salary for surveying and mapping technicians is about $30,400 a year, with the top 10 percent making more than $51,000 a year.

Many surveyors specialize in one area. Boundary surveyors establish and check property lines and construction surveyors help lay out construction sites. Marine or hydrographic surveyors use high-tech gear to measure land under water, while a geographic information specialist uses sophisticated Geographic Information Systems (GIS) software to analyze geographic databases.

Surveyors are often employed by architectural and engineering firms that provide surveying and mapping data to clients. They also frequently work for local, state, and federal government agencies, such as the U.S. Army Corps of Engineers, the U.S. Forest Service, and local urban and redevelopment agencies.

On the Job

Surveying teams go out in the field to gather the information they need to set accurate boundaries. The party chief, who is usually a surveyor or senior surveying technician, leads a team that includes surveying technicians and helpers. The technicians adjust and operate various surveying instruments. For example, they position and hold the vertical rods, or targets, that help the surveyor measure angles, distances, and elevations. They also operate the *theodolite*, which measures horizontal and vertical angles, and the *total station*, which measures and calculates both angles and distances. Surveying technicians carry survey instruments, collect information, perform computations, and create computer-aided drawings. Sometimes helpers come along to help clear brush from the site line, drive stakes in the ground, and carry equipment.

Keys to Success

To succeed as a surveyor, one should have or be

- physically fit
- good with details

🔑 good eyesight

🔑 solid research skills

🔑 a team player

🔑 strong communication skills

Do You Have What It Takes?

To be a surveyor, you must be able to visualize objects, distances, sizes, and abstract forms. Mistakes can be costly, so it's imperative that you work with precision and accuracy. You have to be strong enough to walk long distances while carrying heavy equipment. The job also requires good eyesight, coordination, and interpersonal skills.

A Typical Day at Work

Surveyors generally work an eight-hour day five days a week; but as with many construction jobs, hours may vary depending on the season and weather. You spend much of the day outdoors, gathering data. Depending on what you're surveying, you may need to walk long distances and climb steep hills, all while lugging heavy equipment.

Once the surveying team reaches the surveying site, the workers set up the equipment needed to record the data. Some surveyors work with traditional tools, such as chains, transits, and plumb lines.

Other surveyors rely on GPS to locate reference points. To do this, a surveyor places a satellite signal receiver on a tripod located at a point he or she wants to measure and places another receiver on a point that's already been identified. The receiver then collects the information from several satellites to determine exactly where the "mystery" point is located. After the data are collected, a surveyor must analyze the information and write a report based on the findings.

How to Break In

The courses you take in high school can help prepare you for a career in surveying. Recommended courses include algebra, geometry, trigonometry, drafting, mechanical drawing, and computer science. Workers who've taken college courses in surveying often can land jobs as technicians or assistants, while those with educational training and job experience can work their way into more senior positions, such as senior survey technicians, party chief, and licensed surveyor.

To be a surveyor, you'll need to be licensed by the state in which you plan to work. The requirements vary from state to state, but generally you'll need to pass a written examination given by the National Council of Examiners for Engineering and Surveying (NCEES) and have a set amount of training and education. Graduates of the surveying course often take a Fundamentals of Surveying examination, and then work under the supervision of an experienced surveyor for another four years. Once you've acquired the required experienced, you can become fully licensed by passing the Principles and Practice of Surveyors Examination.

Joining a student chapter of a professional organization in your field can help you reach your goals. Not only will it give you a chance to learn about the field from other professionals, but also the contacts you make may lead to a good job.

Two-Year Training

Look for a community college or trade school that provides two-year programs in surveying and surveying technology. While in school, you'll learn to prepare subdivision and site plans, operate high-tech survey equipment, and conduct topographical and boundary surveys. You'll also learn how to lead field crews and acquire data with GPS devices.

Some students choose to specialize: Possible career paths include construction surveying, boundary surveying, mining surveying, and easement surveying.

To become a licensed surveyor in most states, you'll have to pass an examination given by the NCEES and meet requirements set by your state's licensing board. States also often require surveyors to have a set amount of education and work experience.

After passing the first required examination, survey employees generally work under an experienced surveyor for several years, and then take another examination to qualify as an official surveyor. Because of the complexity of surveying work, many workers choose to continue their education while working in the field. Workers can elect to take specific courses or pursue a bachelor's degree in the field.

What to Look For in a School

When considering a two-year school, be sure to ask these questions:

☞ Does the school offer related course work, such as site design, boundary resolution, and subdivision design?

☞ Does the school provide the latest information on the use of GPS devices for data collection?

☞ Does the school provide co-op opportunities in which students can gain on-the-job training?

☞ What is the school's job placement rate?

☞ What are the instructors' credentials? Have they worked in the industry?

☞ Does the school offer the tools needed for hands-on learning?

☞ Is the school accredited by the Accreditation Board for Engineering and Technology?

☞ Does the school offer management, finance, and other business classes for students who eventually want to start their own businesses?

> **"I have always enjoyed the outdoors. I was in Boy Scouts as a kid. I grew up in a very small town. I don't see myself being inside at all."**
> —Bryant Abt, surveying crew chief

The Future

The demand for professional surveyors with college training and strong technical skills will be good. Some states are starting to require four-year degrees in surveying, so two-year graduates eventually may need to continue their schooling. Workers who are skilled in working with new technologies, such as GPS and GIS, will have a competitive advantage

Did You Know?

George Washington worked as a surveyor for a company that explored western lands. Other famous surveyors include Abraham Lincoln, who worked as a surveyor while studying law; and writer Henry David Thoreau, who supplemented his income as a land surveyor.

Job Seeking Tips

See the suggestions below and turn to Appendix A for advice on creating a résumé, interviewing for schools or jobs, and collecting references.

✔ Decide what you're interested in and seek relevant experience.

✔ Seek advice from the career placement office.

✔ Reach out, and when possible, join associations in your chosen field.

✔ Obtain certification from the National Society of Professional Surveyors.

Interview with a Professional:
Q&A
Bryant Abt

Surveying crew chief, One-Eleven Engineering and
Surveying, Independence, Kentucky

Q: *How did you get started?*

A: My uncle owns a surveying company. I started back in high school. I worked with him. I didn't like surveying at first but eventually I got into it. I like being outside, experiencing nature. I didn't want to be cooped up in an office all the time; I decided I wanted to be outdoors. So I went to Cincinnati State (to earn an associate degree in civil engineering). Basically, I learned a lot of law dealing with boundaries, dealing with the math side of it, lots of ethics, how to be professional, how to manage companies.

Q: *What's a typical day like?*

A: 8 to 4. Eight hours a day. Most of the time, we're pretty busy. I'm outside doing surveying work, going out in the woods doing boundary surveys. Also, we go out on construction sites, where we'll lay out sewers (so construction workers know where the sewers go).

I'm a crew chief. I manage a crew of two to three people. I run a total station. Others run the rod, where you walk around and stake things out. Lots of times, I check maps; I'll sit down and do a lot of drawings and maps. On a construction site, I check the engineering work. I do a quality control check to make sure everything is done right before it's put in. On boundary surveys, lots of times I do research beforehand to figure out where property lines are.

It's not a monotonous job at all. There's always something different you're doing day in and day out.

Q: *What's your advice for people starting a career?*

A: Make sure you have the money squared up for college; that's the biggest thing. Get a good education. You have to have that education. Otherwise you are going nowhere in the construction field.

Q: *What's the best part about being a surveyor?*

A: The professionalism. Everybody is very straightforward with each other. They help each other out. They help resolve issues in the field.

Career Connections

For more information on surveying careers, contact the following organizations.

American Congress on Surveying and Mapping http://www.acsm.net

National Society of Professional Surveyors http://www .surveyingcareer.com

Land Surveyor Reference Page http://www.lsrp.com/proforg.html

American Land Title Association http://www.alta.org

American Council for Construction Education http://www .acce-hq.org

National Center for Construction Education and Research http://www.nccer.org

Construct My Future http://www.ConstructMyFuture.com

Associate's Degree Programs

Here are a few schools with two-year surveying programs:

Mohawk Valley Community College, Utica, New York

The University of Akron–Community and Technical College, Akron, Ohio

Greenville Technical College, Greenville, South Carolina

Pennsylvania College of Technology, Williamsport, Pennsylvania

Financial Aid

Turn to Appendix B for more on financial aid for two-year students.

The American Congress on Surveying and Mapping (ACSM) provides scholarships to students studying surveying, mapping, geographic information systems, and geodetic science programs. http://www.acsm.net/scholar.html

The National Society of Professional Surveyors gives TRIG_STAR awards to high school trigonometry students who finish first in competitions involving the practical application of trigonometry. http://www.nspsmo.org/trig_star/scholarship.shtml

Related Careers

Civil engineer, architect, and landscape architect.

Civil Engineering Technician

Vital Statistics

Salary: Civil engineering technicians earn a median annual income of about $38,500 a year with the top 10 percent earning more than $57,500 a year, according to 2006 data from the U.S. Bureau of Labor Statistics. Civil engineers typically earn $51,000 to $80,000 a year.

Employment: Civil engineering technicians with an associate's degree and on-the-job training will be in demand. Job prospects for licensed civil engineers also are good. Employment in the field through 2014 is forecast to grow about as fast as the average for all occupations, according to the Bureau of Labor Statistics.

Education: A two-year degree program in civil engineering technology will prepare you for a career as a civil engineering technician. A bachelor's degree coupled with work experienced generally is needed to become a fully licensed civil engineer.

Work Environment: Civil engineering technicians and civil engineers work both indoors and out. On some days, they work in the office, preparing drawings, estimating construction costs, and ordering materials. On other days, they go out to the site, where they oversee the plans for the construction or rebuilding of highways, buildings, dams, bridges, and sewers.

Whenever you fly into an airport, visit a sports stadium, or drive down a highway, you're enjoying a structure made possible by the vision of a civil engineer. Civil engineers plan and build everything from roads and bridges to sports stadiums and public buildings. Their vision has helped produce some of the world's great wonders, including the construction of the Hoover Dam, the Brooklyn Bridge, and the Panama Canal.

Civil engineering technicians play a vital role in helping design and build these projects. They estimate construction costs, research the projects, specify the needed materials, and prepare drawings. They work as cost estimators, project managers, and schedulers.

Civil engineering projects have three stages: In the preconstruction stage, you survey the land, review plans, order materials, hire the staff, and estimate how much the project will cost and how long it will take to finish.

The next stage occurs when the actual work begins. During the construction phrase, you spend much of your time at the site, overseeing the work, spotting problems, and quickly working to fix them.

The final stage—infrastructure maintenance—occurs once the project is done. Your role is to wrap up the loose ends, such as finishing needed paperwork and making final adjustments to the structure.

About 94,000 civil engineering technicians are employed in the United States. The median annual salary for civil engineering technicians varies depending on where they work: Technicians in local government make about $43,700 a year, employees working for architectural and engineering firms make about $37,500, and those working for the state government earn about $36,000 a year. The top 10 percent of wage earners in the field make more than $57,500 a year.

About 237,000 people work as civil engineers in the United States. Of those, about half work for firms that provide architectural, engineering, and similar services. Other engineers typically work for the government or in the construction industry. Civil engineers often specialize. Many work as construction engineers who oversee major building projects. Others civil engineers work in environmental, geo-technical, structural, and transportation areas.

The average starting salary for a full-fledged civil engineer with a bachelor's degree is about $44,000. The top 10 percent wage earners make more than $94,600 a year.

On the Job

Civil engineers and civil engineering technicians design everything from roads and buildings to airports and water supplies. They use their creativity and engineering skills to create structures that are safe, economical, and sturdy enough to withstand the test of time and the forces of nature. When planning a structure, they're responsible for picking the best materials, controlling costs, and allowing enough time to successfully complete the project.

During the planning stages, they often work inside their offices, researching the project, estimating costs, preparing drawings, creating schedules, and choosing materials. Once a project is under way, they travel to the site, where they oversee the work. If emergencies come up—and they almost always do—they're charged with quickly figuring out solutions so the work can continue.

Once a structure is completed, civil engineering workers test it to make sure everything has been properly constructed—whether it is a highway, bridge, public garage, or other structure. They also must complete all the required paperwork, whether it is a bill from a contractor or an application for a certificate of occupancy.

 Keys to Success

To be a successful civil engineer, you need
- creativity
- excellent math skills

- organization
- good communication skills
- analytical ability
- problem-solving ability
- attention to detail

Do You Have What It Takes?

To work as a civil engineer or civil engineering technician, you need to be a math whiz, have a creative streak, and be a problem solver. Because you'll need to work with a variety of clients and workers, good communication skills are vital. You should also have an interest in helping the public, since most civil engineering projects are designed to benefit the general public.

A Typical Day at Work

Depending on the status of a project, someone working in civil engineering may work indoors or out. During the planning stage, you often work in the office, doing research, estimating costs, preparing drawings, writing up contracts, securing materials, and lining up contractors for the job. You may go to the site to test the soil or concrete to see if it's suitable for the planned construction.

Once the job begins, you spend much of your time on the construction site, where you'll oversee the work. If the project is far away from your home, you may have to set up a temporary residence near the site. During the building stage, your job is to oversee the project—making sure the project is being built properly and that the work is staying within the allotted budget and time frame. If a problem arises—a storm that throws the project behind schedule or an overlooked building code—your job is to quickly find a solution.

The demands of the project dictate your hours. When the project is going smoothly, you may be able to work a typical 40-hour work week. When deadlines are looming or unexpected problems crop up, you may end up putting in long hours that extend into weekends and holidays.

How to Break In

You can get a head start on a career in civil engineering while still in high school. Courses that will prepare you to work in this field include plane geometry, physics, chemistry, geometry, trigonometry, calculus, and computer science.

Now is a good time to start reading about civil engineering: Good choices include engineering magazines, business sections in newspapers, and books that describe amazing engineering feats. Not only will these publications pique your interest about your chosen field, but the knowledge you gain will come in handy once you start working as an engineer.

Gaining relevant work experience will also give you an edge. While in high school, you can pick up valuable experience in related industries, by working as an assistant on a survey team, as part of a soil checking crew, or as a worker on a construction site. After you start college, you can gain even more experience as an intern at an engineering firm. Becoming an active member of a professional association, such as the American Society of Certified Engineering Technicians (http://www.ascet.org), can help you make important contacts that can lead to internships and, eventually, a real job.

You also should work to become certified by The National Institute for Certification of Engineering Technologies (http://www.nicet.org). To become certified in one of its various specialties, you must pass a written examination and provide proof of job-related experience, a supervisor's evaluation, and a letter of recommendation. Doing so will show potential employers that you've acquired the skills needed to do the job.

"It's not a glamorous field but you hear all the time about bridges that are closed and roads that need to be repaired and sewers that are getting old. There's a whole lot of infrastructure that needs be done. Civil engineers are guaranteed work for the rest of their lives."
—Pam Dullum, forensics civil engineer

Two-Year Training

Technical institutes, community colleges, vocational-technical schools, the armed forces, and extension divisions at colleges and universities often provide programs in engineering technology.

Of these, about 230 offer engineering technology programs that have been accredited by the Technology Accreditation Commission of the Accreditation Board for Engineering and Technology (ABET) (http://www. abet.org/). Such schools require students to take a minimum of college algebra, trigonometry, and one or two basic science courses.

Before choosing a program, it's important to carefully consider your long-range plans and the college's offerings. For example, if you enroll in a two-year pre-engineering program, and then decide not to pursue a four-year degree, you may have a hard time finding a job as an engineering technician, because the course work in the first two years focuses more on academics than hands-on training. Likewise, if you receive a two-year degree in engineering technology, and later decide to get a bachelor's degree in civil engineering, you may not be able to transfer all of your credits.

What to Look For in a School

When considering a two-year school, be sure to ask these questions:

☞ Does the school offer related course work in subjects such as mathematics, science, and technology?

☞ Can the school help you find an internship in which you can get-on-the-job training?

☞ What is the school's job placement rate?

☞ What are the instructors' credentials? Have they worked in the industry?

☞ Is the school accredited by the Accreditation Board for Engineering and Technology?

☞ If you hope to someday pursue a bachelor's degree in civil engineering, are the credits you earn in the associate program transferable to a four-year program?

The Future

The nation's infrastructure—its bridges, highways, sewers, and public buildings—are in need of repair, making the job outlook for skilled civil engineers and civil engineering technicians bright. Those with high-tech training and skills will be in especially high demand.

Did You Know?

The construction of the Panama Canal is still considered an amazing engineering and construction feat. To create the canal, 211 million cubic yards of earth had to be removed. That's enough dirt to fill more than 70 million pick-up trucks. (Source: The Junior Engineering Technical Society.)

Interview with a Professional:
Q&A
Pam Dullum

Forensic civil engineer, Gervasio & Associates Inc.,
Phoenix, Arizona

Q: *How did you get started?*

A: I got interested in high school when I was taking physics. I loved physics and math, and asked my teacher, "What can I do so I can do physics for the rest of my life?" My high school physics teacher said, "Become an engineer."

I got accepted in the University of Minnesota in a civil engineering program. At that time I was interested in going in the service and going through the ROTC program. I was a scholarship student. They paid for school. I went for school nine months of the year and each summer I spent six weeks of summer training with the navy. Between by junior and senior year, I was sent out to work with a civil engineer.

Q: *What's a typical day like?*

A: I work 9 a.m. to 6 p.m. I spend about 80 percent of my time in the office. In forensics engineering, I' m primarily doing investigations. A typical day runs the gamut from sitting in my office reading cases to putting together a presentation for a project. A two- or three-year construction project will have a lot of paperwork.

I also have days when I go out in the field. I may have to do a site visit when a homeowner has a drainage problem that they think is being caused by a neighbor. I go out and investigate to find out what is causing the problem.

When I worked as a construction engineer, I typically worked from 7 a.m. to 4 p.m. I spent probably 85 percent of my time in the field and 15 percent of my time in the office doing paperwork.

Q: *What's your advice for people starting a career?*

A: Take as rigorous a college prep in high school as you can, preferably with physics and calculus. It's not an easy curriculum in college, so you have to be willing to work at it.

Pursue working with a civil engineering firm. There are a lot of different jobs in civil engineering that you can do without a degree in civil engineering. Soil testing firms hire high school graduates. You learn to test soils and how to test concrete. Certainly working on a survey team is a good experience. The construction industry is always looking for people to work in the trades. It's a way to make money toward college and get a view of what goes on in construction.

Q: What's the best part about being a civil engineer?

A: The ability to work toward a goal and step away and look at something tangible for years afterward and being able to say I helped built that. I worked on the Denver International Airport, and there's not a time that I go there that I don't look around with pride.

Job Seeking Tips

See the suggestions below and turn to Appendix A for advice on creating a résumé, interviewing for schools or jobs, and collecting references.

✔ Decide what you're interested in and seek relevant experience.

✔ Seek advice from the career placement office.

✔ Reach out, and when possible, join professional associations, such as the American Society of Certified Engineering Technicians (http://www.ascet.org), the Junior Engineering Technical Society (http://www.jets.org), and the Accreditation Board for Engineering and Technology (http://www.abet.org).

✔ Look for opportunities to work as a summer intern or part-time worker with a civil engineering firm, surveying team, or construction crew.

Career Connections

For more information on civil engineering careers, contact the following organizations.

American Society of Certified Engineering Technicians http://www.ascet.org

Junior Engineering Technical Society http://www.jets.org

Accreditation Board for Engineering and Technology http://www.abet.org

National Institute for Certification of Engineering Technology http://www.nicet.org

Society of Women Engineers http://www.societyofwomenengineers.org

Civil Engineering Jobs http://www.civilengineeringjobs.com

Pathways to Technology http://www.pathwaystotechnology.org

Associate's Degree Programs

Here are a few schools with two-year civil engineering programs:

The University of Akron, Community and Technical College, Akron, Ohio

Bluefield State College, Bluefield, West Virginia

Pellissippi State Technical Community College, Knoxville, Tennessee

Pennsylvania College of Technology, Williamsport, Pennsylvania

Southwest Tennessee Community College, Memphis, Tennessee

Wake Technical Community College, Raleigh, North Carolina

Financial Aid

Here are a few civil engineering–related scholarships. Turn to Appendix B for more on financial aid for two-year students.

Joseph C. Johnson Memorial Grant is awarded to qualified engineering technology students. http://www.ascet.org

The Joseph M. Parish Memorial Grant goes to student members of the ASCET who are enrolled in an engineering technology program and demonstrate financial need. http://www.ascet.org

ASCET awards small cash grants to ASCET college students who are studying engineering technology and high school students who plan to study engineering technology. http://www.ascet.org

Related Careers

Cost estimator, drafter, surveyor, cartographer, surveying technician, science technician, engineering manager, sales engineer, engineering technician, and architect.

Construction Site Manager

Vital Statistics

Salary: The median average annual salary for construction managers is about $70,000, according to 2006 data from the the U.S. Bureau of Labor Statistics, and people starting out in trades that can lead to this specialty earn $15 to $20 an hour—or $31,000 to $42,000 a year.

Employment: The demand is high for construction managers with a solid education in relevant subject areas, hands-on experience in construction, and strong communication skills in English and Spanish. Through 2014 employment in the profession is expected to grow as fast as the average for all occupations, according to the Bureau of Labor Statistics.

Education: A two-year degree in construction management coupled with work experience in the construction industry can help you gain a foothold in this field.

Work Environment: Construction managers work both indoors and outdoors. Sometimes they work from a main office, where they keep tabs on ongoing projects; other times they work at construction sites.

Pity the Three Little Pigs. When they tried to build new homes, they didn't have a construction manager to make sure their buildings could withstand the huffing and puffing of a big bad wolf.

Today construction workers face much better odds. Whether they're building a new house, giant shopping mall, or section of a highway, construction workers rely on the expertise of a construction manager who oversees the building project from start to finish.

Depending on the complexity of the plan, a construction manager may oversee the entire project or just a piece of it. Many managers specialize, focusing on a specific category, such as the construction of new homes, commercial buildings, bridges, or roads.

As a construction manager, you estimate how much a project will cost, line up the required building permits, order the needed materials, and schedule work loads. Depending on your role, you also may be in charge of hiring carpenters, painters, plumbers, electricians, and other workers for the project. While the building is under construction, you must keep an eye on costs, enforce safety rules, monitor the work to make sure it's being done correctly, and try your best to keep the project running on time. To do all this well, you have to be a master juggler who can manage multiple tasks and competing interests all at once. You also must be able to work under pressure and know how to communicate with both force and tact.

Construction managers are commonly referred to by other titles, including construction supervisor, general contractor, and constructor. No matter the title, managers in the construction industry generally are well paid. The median salary for the approximately 430,000 construction managers in the United States is about $70,000. The top 10 percent earn more than $126,000 each year. More than half of all construction managers are self-employed, with many owning their own construction firms.

Because the construction industry is so complex, education and on-the-job training are essential. To that end, community colleges and trade schools with construction management programs often give students the opportunity to gain work experience while in school. Not only will these work-study experiences give you much needed job skills, but they can lead to permanent jobs after you earn your associate's degree.

Graduates in construction management rarely start out overseeing an entire project on their own. Instead, they hone their skills working under a more experienced manager as an assistant to a project manager, field engineer, or cost estimator. Those who seek more formal training can pursue a bachelor's or master's degree, often while working—and earning money— in construction management.

On the Job

As a construction manager, your task is to make sure a construction job is done properly, on time and within the allotted budget. To make sure all of this happens, a manager keeps tabs on a project from start to finish. He estimates costs, schedules the work, orders supplies, secures building permits, and oversees the employees.

Depending on the day, a manager sometimes works from his office and stays in touch with workers at the construction site via cell phone and e-mail. She or he is often on the phone, talking to customers, suppliers, government officials, and others involved in the building of a new structure.

The manager also frequently travels to the site, where she or he can oversee the work—making sure tools are being used correctly, safety rules are being followed, the construction is being done properly, and the work is moving at a reasonable pace.

> **"It's important to admit when you don't know something. Sometimes you simply don't know the answer and you have to research it. It's better to make an informed decision than a quick seat-of-the-pants decision."**
> —Christine J. Flaherty, construction manager

Keys to Success

For success as a construction site manager, you should have

- good communication skills in English, and Spanish is helpful
- strong computer skills
- construction experience
- solid math skills
- the ability to work under pressure
- management skills

Do You Have What It Takes?

To be a construction manager, you need to be able to juggle tasks and demands while making sure the project is finished on time and within the allotted budget. Being able to communicate what needs to be done to workers and clients is critical. Extensive hands-on experience in construction coupled with solid skills in math, computers, and building design are essential.

A Typical Day at Work

For a construction manager, there's no such thing as a typical work day. That's because construction managers are often on call 24 hours a day. If there's an emergency at the site, the manager is the first one to get the call. If weather delays or other unforeseen problems put a project behind schedule, the construction manager must get it back on track, even if it means working long days, on weekends, and even on holidays.

When working in an office, the construction manager makes sure paperwork is filled out correctly, oversees estimates, double-checks supply orders, and handles queries from customers and workers at the site.

At the construction site, the manager checks the work to make sure the project is being completed on time and within the estimated budget. She or he also oversees the workers—making sure they follow safety rules, use the proper tools, and do the job right the first time. If there's a problem—whether a shortage of plywood, the wrong size pipe, or a missing permit—the manager must solve the problem quickly without jeopardizing the integrity of the project.

How to Break In

While you're in high school, seek summer and weekend jobs that will expose you to the different aspects of construction. Whether you're helping paint houses on the weekends or loading supplies for a building contractor, you'll gain first-hand knowledge about the industry.

After high school, you can further enhance your skills by enrolling in a two-year program in construction management at a school that provides cooperative relationships with building contractors. While in school and on the job, you'll learn how to estimate the costs of different projects, design projects on a computer, perform inspections, and schedule building activities. You'll also have a chance to learn local building codes.

To improve your marketability, you should work to become certified by the American Institute of Constructors (http://www.aicnet.org) or the Construction Management Association of America (http://www.cmaanet.org). Being certified shows potential employers that you've met the standards needed (education, examinations, experience) to work in this field.

Becoming an active student member in professional organizations, such as the Home Builders Institute and the American Institute of Contractors, also can help. Not only will you have a chance to pick up helpful suggestions from future colleagues in the organizations, but those contacts could very well help you land your first job.

Two-Year Training

Many community colleges and trade schools offer two-year programs that can help prepare you for a career in construction management. While in school, you'll take a variety of courses, such as algebra, trigonometry, construction estimating, English composition, surveying measurements, civil engineering, computer-assisted design (CAD), and site drafting. Some schools also offer courses in Spanish to help managers communicate with the growing number of Spanish-speaking construction workers.

Because on-the-job training is so essential in this field, schools often offer co-op programs with employers. Trainees learn a variety of skills, including how to estimate projects, schedule workloads, and perform inspections.

What to Look For in a School

When considering a two-year school, be sure to ask these questions:

☞ Does the school offer related course work, such as cost estimation, architectural drafting, and surveying measurements?

☞ Does the school provide the latest information on local building codes?

☞ Will the school provide co-op opportunities in which students gain on-the-job training?

☞ What is the school's job placement rate?

☞ What are the instructors' credentials? Have they worked in the industry?

☞ Does the school offer the tools needed for hands-on learning?

☞ Does the school offer management, finance, and other business classes for students who eventually want to start their own businesses?

The Future

The demand for construction managers with educational training and hands-on experience in the field is expected to be high. Because of the growing number of Spanish-speaking workers, managers who can speak both English and Spanish will be in especially high demand.

Did You Know?

A widow's fear of ghosts turned what could have been a simple construction project into one that lasted 38 years—qualifying the Winchester House in San Jose, California, for the "Longest Continuous House Construction" in the Guinness World Records. After the death of her husband, the widowed Sarah Winchester (heiress to the Winchester rifle fortune), turned the family's eight-room farmhouse into a mystery house with closets that opened into blank walls and stairways leading to nowhere. Some think she did so to appease and confuse all the ghosts killed by the "gun that won the West."

Job Seeking Tips

See the suggestions below and turn to Appendix A for advice on creating a résumé, interviewing for schools or jobs, and collecting references.

✔ Decide what you're interested in and seek relevant experience.

✔ Seek advice from the career placement office.

✔ Join student chapters of professional associations, such as the Home Builders Institute (http://www.hbi.org) and the American Institute of Constructors (http://www.aicnet.org).

✔ Obtain certification from professional groups, such as the American Institute of Constructors (http://www.aicnet.org) and the Construction Management Association of America (http://www.cmaanet.org).

Interview with a Professional:
Q&A

Christine J. Flaherty

Certified construction manager/business development
manager, STV Construction Inc., New York, New York

Q: *How did you get started?*

A: I majored in civil engineering. I was always interested in going out in the
field to see how things worked. I found a small firm that placed you based
on your interests and talents into different things. They were advocates of
giving you a good bit of responsibility early on and providing a mentor.

I worked on my first construction site after graduation. I ended up at a
campus and was put in a position of project manager. I was lucky to have a
good, strong team that mentored me.

Q: *What's a typical day like?*

A: For a project manager, a typical day requires a lot of communication
with people. From contractors to tradesmen to owners and clients who are
concerned about their clients, there are people you need to keep informed
about what's going on with their projects.

If you're working on a construction site, the first thing you need to do is
make sure the project is moving the way it was planned for that morning.
Check in with the individual workers, making sure there are not any im-
mediate problems. There probably will be a field condition, or challenge in
the drawings that will require attention or answers so the constructors can
continue work. You have to work with the architects and engineers to find
solutions. You have to deal with the budget ramifications. What's the cost
impact? The time impact of these changes? You'll be going to client meetings, updating the client on different things concerning the project. You'll
be dealing with pay applications from the contractors, making sure it's the
right dollar amount.

Q: *What's your advice for those starting a career?*

A: Once you find a job, it's important to remember that there are no stupid
questions. Find people around you who are willing to be mentors. Find
people who are willing to answer questions. It doesn't have to be your
manager; it can be the carpenter foremen on your project. There's always
something to learn from everyone on the project, whether it's a technical
detail or something about leadership and management.

(continued on next page)

(continued from previous page)

Figure out the types of goals you have, observe the people around you who are excelling at things you want to succeed in. Find ways to pick up characteristics and things they do that work well for them.

If you're aggressive in learning while you're working, you will succeed faster because you're showing initiative and you're showing that you care about your own career.

Q: *What's the best part of being a construction manager?*

A: I love watching buildings getting built. It's very exciting seeing a building put together. I'm a people person. I love that I work with all sorts of people with different backgrounds, different experiences, and different crafts. They all come together for a project and they all are able to create something.

As construction manager, I play a key role in that process. It's very rewarding. You can look back and know you were part of a team that built or improved a facility. That's tangible. You can look back and say, "I was part of it."

Career Connections

For more information on careers in construction management, contact the following organizations.

American Institute of Constructors http://www.aicnet.org

Construction Management Association of America http://www.cmaanet.org

American Council for Construction Education http://www.acce-hq.org

National Center for Construction Education and Research http://www.nccer.org

Construct My Future http://www.ConstructMyFuture.com

The Home Builders Institute http://www.hbi.org

Associate's Degree Programs

Here are few schools that offer two-year degrees in construction management:

Santa Fe Community College, Gainesville, Florida

Cincinnati State Technical & Community College, Cincinnati, Ohio

North Lake College, Dallas, Texas

State Fair Community College, Seldalia, Missouri

New York City Technical College, Brooklyn, New York

Financial Aid

Here are a few scholarships related to construction management. Turn to Appendix B for more on financial aid for two-year students.

Construction Management Association Foundation awards scholarships to students enrolled in accredited construction management programs. Candidates must have completed one full year to be eligible. http://www.cmaanet.org/scholarships.php

The National Housing Endowment oversees numerous scholarships for students pursuing degrees in the construction industry. http://www.nationalhousingendowment.com/Scholarships.htm

The National Association of Women in Construction (NAWIC) Atlanta Scholarship Foundation awards scholarships to students enrolled in a construction degree program with at least one-term remaining toward their constructed-related degree. http://www.nawicatlanta.org

Related Careers

Architect, civil engineer, cost estimator, landscape architect, engineering manager, and natural science manager.

Interior Designer

Vital Statistics

Salary: The median annual salary for interior designers is about $40,700, with the top 10 percent making more than $72,000 a year, according to 2006 data from the U.S. Bureau of Labor Statistics.

Employment: The job outlook for skilled commercial interior designers who work and communicate well with their clients is good. Job growth in the field is expected to rise as fast as the average for all occupations through 2014, according to the Bureau of Labor Statistics.

Education: A two-year training program at a design school or college, coupled with an apprenticeship, can ready you for a career in commercial interior design.

Work Environment: Commercial interior designers work in their own offices or studios. They also go to showrooms, design centers, and trade shows to select products and gather design ideas.

The design of a company's indoor space can make—or break —a business. A well-laid-out store spurs shoppers to spend money, while a poorly designed one may very well chase them away. Likewise, a smartly designed workplace improves worker productivity and satisfaction. And a well-appointed resort leaves clients feeling pampered, increasing the odds they'll come back.

Knowing how to achieve such results requires an artistic eye, good business sense, strong communication skills, and a solid understanding of design. To be a good designer, you need to be flexible and imaginative enough to make your clients happy. You have to be able to listen to their needs and then come up with a workable design that meets their budget and time demands. Do they want exposed wooden floors, track lighting, modern furniture, or built-in bookshelves, for example?

Enrolling in a two-year program at a design school or a college that offers design classes will provide you with the basics. You also will need to spend one to three years working as an apprentice under the supervision of a skilled designer.

Once you've completed your initial education and training, you can take a national licensing examination. While not all states require interior design licenses, having one helps establish you as a professional who deserves the trust of potential employers.

About 65,000 people work as interior designers in the United States. Of those, about 30 percent are self-employed. Designers also work for design firms, architects, landscape architects, and home furnishing stores.

As a commercial designer, you may be asked to design the interior space of an office, store, restaurant, or nightclub. Not only will you develop a layout for the space, but also you'll work with the owner to choose the colors, furnishings, lighting, and overall design style for the business. On larger projects, such as office complexes and school buildings, you may be in charge of locating the best spots for walkways, stairs, and elevators. During the course of the project, you'll keep the client updated on any changes or unforeseen obstacles. Depending on the job, you may need to work with architects, engineers, and electricians to make sure your designs are safe and meet the local building codes.

Experienced interior designers are often well paid. The median annual salary is about $40,700, with top earners making more than $71,200 a year.

Designers' fees for commercial projects vary. Depending on the situation, they may charge a flat rate for the entire project, charge by the square footage, or charge by the hour. In addition, designers often get a percentage of the money paid to the contractors they hire to do the actual work.

Of course, the money is important; but for many interior designers, the true satisfaction comes from transforming a chaotic workspace into a smooth operation that's both aesthetically pleasing and functional. What's the ultimate reward? When the client looks at what you've done and says, "Wow!"

On the Job

As an interior designer, you'll spend much of your day communicating with others. When you're working with a new client, you must listen carefully and ask follow-up questions to fully understand what the client needs. Using this information, your job is to come up with a plan that fits those needs and do so within the client's budget and time frame.

When you show the client a preliminary sketch, it's your job to explain why the plan meets your client's needs and, if necessary, come up with viable alternatives. Once a client signs off on the initial plan, you get to develop more detailed drawings and specifications. As you work on the plan, you'll need to stay in touch with the client to make sure he or she understands—and approves—the plans.

When the project is under way, your job is to make sure the work turns out the way you and the client envisioned it. During the process, you'll work with painters, electricians, carpet installers, and other contractors who will help bring your design to life.

Keys to Success

To succeed as an interior designer, you need

🔑 an artistic eye

❧ imagination
❧ good communication skills
❧ flexibility
❧ self-discipline
❧ business sense
❧ problem-solving ability

Do You Have What It Takes?

To be a good designer, you need to be flexible and imaginative enough to make your clients happy. You need to be able to listen to their needs, and then come up with a workable design that meets their needs, budget, and time constraints. If you enjoy decorating your own room—moving furniture around, painting the walls, putting up posters, and trying out different lighting—you might have what it takes to be a designer.

A Typical Day at Work

A commercial interior designer is often at the beck and call of his or her clients. When and where you work depends largely on what your client needs. Designers who work for a large corporation or design firm often work regular hours in comfortable offices. Those who work for small design firms or themselves typically work around their clients' schedule, meeting them on site during the evening, early in the morning, or even on a weekend.

If a project is just getting under way, you'll meet with the client to learn what kind of design work they're seeking, how much money they can spend, and how quickly they need the job completed. Before you draw up the plans, you'll visit the site—whether a restaurant, office park, or school—where you'll assess the existing space, furniture, and equipment. You'll then come up with a proposed plan that meets your client's design goals and budget needs. Depending on the complexity of the project, you may produce hand-sketched drawings or create computer-aided designs.

After you and the client have agreed on the plan, you can start selecting specific materials, furniture, artwork, and wall coverings for the project. You may also need to check with a construction inspector to make sure the project meets required building codes, and hire contractors to install new lighting, plumbing, and electrical fixtures.

Once the work starts, it's your job to make sure the project progresses smoothly while meeting agreed-upon deadlines and staying within the allotted budget.

How to Break In

While in school, you can become a student member the American Society of Interior Designers (http://www.asid.org/), which will help you meet others in the field, and may even help you land a dream apprenticeship. Apprenticeships, which usually last one to three years, are designed to give you the experience you'll need to qualify as a fully licensed designer. Depending on your interests, you might end up working in a design firm, architectural firm, or furniture store. To make sure you receive the proper training, the Interior Design Experience Program (IDEP) will oversee the apprenticeship program and also provide mentoring and workshop opportunities.

After you complete your apprenticeship, you'll be eligible to take a national licensing examination given by The National Council of Interior Design (http://www.ncidq.org/). The National Kitchen and Bath Association (http://www.nkba.org/) also offers certification for kitchen and bath designers.

> "People perceive interior design as a creative field. They say, 'Oh, [you] get to be creative.' In reality, it's a creative response to a need. Your creativity is tapped in the fact that you're coming up with a creative solution."
> —Bruce Goff, interior designer

Two-Year Training

Enrolling in a two-year program in a professional design school or college can get you started on the right career path. While in school, you'll take a variety of courses, such as furniture design, architecture, spatial planning, ergonomics, ethics, and even psychology. Because of the growing use of computers in the design field, you'll also be required to learn how to work with computer-aided design (CAD) software.

Students who enroll in a two- or three-year program will earn a certificate or an associate's degree in interior design, which will prepare them to work as assistants to interior designers, space planners, and consultants in furniture stores.

Students who want to further their education can pursue a bachelor's degree in the field.

What to Look For in a School

When considering a two-year school, be sure to ask these questions:

☞ Does the school offer related course work in subjects such as color and design, spatial planning, and CAD?

☞ Can the school help you find an apprenticeship in which you can get-on-the-job training?

☞ What is the school's job placement rate?

☞ What are the instructors' credentials? Have they worked in the industry?

☞ Does the school offer the tools needed for hands-on learning?

☞ Does the school offer management, finance, and other business classes for students who eventually want to start their own businesses?

☞ Is the school accredited or affiliated with a professional association, such as the National Association of School of Art and Design, or the Foundation for Interior Design Education Research?

The Future

Talented designers with the proper educational training and experience will be in demand. Designers who specialize in growth areas, such as ergonomic designs, elder designs, and environmentally friendly designs, may be able to establish profitable niche-businesses.

Did You Know?

As owner of an interior-design business, Grace Adler (played by Debra Messing) on NBC's sitcom *Will & Grace* made interior design work in Manhattan look glamorous and at times downright silly.

Job Seeking Tips

See the suggestions below and turn to Appendix A for advice on creating a résumé, interviewing for schools or jobs, and collecting references.

✔ Decide what you're interested in and seek relevant experience.

✔ Seek advice from the career placement office.

✔ Reach out and, when possible, join associations in your chosen field.

✔ Develop a portfolio that shows off your best work. If possible, include designs for a variety of projects.

Interview with a Professional:
Q&A
Bruce Goff
Principal of Domus Design Group, San Francisco, California

Q: *How did you get started?*

A: The usual joke in my family was I started moving the furniture around in my house around age two. In preschool, my teacher called my mother up and asked for a conference. My mother comes in and sits down, and this woman says, "We have one little problem with Bruce. He keeps getting all the other kids to get up and rearrange the way the activity floor is set up. He wants to change where the toys are."

You might say that's the way I look at things. I like problem solving. I'm always intrigued by how to make things better. That's our corporate logo: "Live better, work smarter."

Q: *What's a typical day like?*

A: The funny thing is there is no typical day, but there are a series of things you typically do. There are client meetings: As an example, this morning I had a 7 a.m. conference call on a project. I was on the phone with the owner, with the superintendent and one of the consultants about issues on the site we discovered. At 8 o'clock, I had a meeting for a new project. At 11, I have a meeting with a client to go over the next fiscal year's worth of projects. I will have this afternoon a meeting with a rep to show us new products. I will be on site on another project in a couple of hours. And in between all that, I'll probably have 9 to 10 phone calls with people on my staff, and a couple of hundred e-mails.

Q: *What's your advice for people starting a career?*

A: First of all you have to like to communicate. You have to communicate effectively. In reality, that's the business we're in. The brilliance of design is only a small part of the equation. Communicating what that design is, communicating how to get it done, communicating about why it should be done is the key. Reading, writing, and speaking are the linchpins.

Q: *What's the best part about being a commercial interior designer?*

A: What makes me still get up at 4 a.m. besides, "Oh my god, I'm behind!"? Today I'm doing something interesting to me. I find chaos and try to leave it organized.

Career Connections

For more information on interior designing careers, contact the following organizations.

American Society of Interior Designers http://www.asid.org

Foundation for Interior Design Education Researchhttp://www
.accredit-id.org/

International Interior Design Association http://www.iida.org

Interior Design Educators Council http://www.idec.org

National Association of Schools of Art and Designhttp://nasad
.arts-accredit.org/

National Council for Interior Design Qualification http://www
.ncidq.org

National Kitchen and Bath Association http://www.nkba.org/student

Interior Design Jobs http://www.InteriorDesignJobs.com

Associate's Degree Programs

Here are a few schools with two-year interior designing programs:

Scottsdale Community College, Scottsdale, Arizona

Brooks College, Long Beach, California

Dakota County Technical College, Rosemount, Minnesota

Joliet Junior College, Joliet, Illinois

Financial Aid

Here are a few scholarships related to interior design. Turn to Appendix B for more information on financial aid for two-year students.

Yale R. Burge Competition offers an award to students with strong portfolios. Students must be in final year of undergraduate study in at least a three-year program of interior design.   http://www.asid.org/asidfoundation

Irene Winifred Eno Grant goes to students and design professionals who create an educational program or interior design research project dedicated to health, safety, and welfare.   http://www.asid.org/asidfoundation

Related Fields

Architect, artist, commercial designer, industry designer, fashion designer, floral designer, graphic designer, landscape architect.

Mason

Concrete is one of those conveniences we take for granted. Whether we're driving on a highway, crossing a bridge, or walking on a sidewalk, concrete is the magic ingredient that provides a strong, smooth surface for our travels. These sturdy structures are created by cement masons and concrete finishers—skilled craftspeople who know how to turn cement, water, sand, and gravel into concrete.

Some concrete workers specialize. Segmental pavers, for example, cut and install flat pieces of compacted concrete or brick to make driveways and paths. Terrazzo workers, on the other hand, use their artistic and masonry skills to create colorful patios, walkways, and floors.

Not all masons work with concrete. Some work with other materials, such as stones and bricks. Stonemasons use marble, granite, cast concrete, and similar materials to build walls, floors, and homes, while brick masons, or bricklayers, use bricks to create fireplaces, homes, and other structures.

To become a mason, you first need to work as an apprentice under the supervision of a skilled journeyman. As an apprentice, you'll spend about three years in an on-the-job training program under the watchful eye of a skilled journeyman. You'll also be required to take at least 144 hours of classroom instruction in blueprint reading, mathematics, layout work, and other subjects. Such courses can often be taken as part of a two-year degree program at a trade school, community college, or technical school.

Skilled masons are in great demand, with highly skilled specialists drawing the best wages. The top 10 percent of cement masons and concrete finishers earn nearly $54,000 a year, while the top 10 percent of stonemasons make more than $56,000 a year. Just be aware that the fickleness of the weather and construction industry can cause fluctuations in pay. During bad weather and construction slowdowns, your earnings could dip; in busy times, overtime hours can dramatically boost your take-home pay.

About 209,000 workers are employed as cement masons, concrete finishers, segmental pavers, and terrazzo workers in the United States. Of these, cement masons and concrete finishers hold the bulk of the jobs. These tradesmen generally work for contractors who specialize in foundations, structures, and building exteriors. They also work on construction teams for residential buildings and major construction projects, such as highways, bridges, schools, and shopping malls.

About 177,000 people work as brick masons, block masons, and stonemasons in the United States, with brick masons making up the biggest category. These tradespeople usually work for contractors; about one-third of them are self-employed.

On the Job

Concrete masons and concrete finishers work outdoors in teams. Before the concrete can even be poured, workers must set and align the forms that will hold the concrete. As the concrete is cast, workers use shovels and tools to spread it. Masons guide a straightedge back and forth across the top to "screed" or level the concrete. Once the concrete is level, they use a long-handled tool called a "bull float" to smooth the surface. After the concrete has been leveled and floated, the finishers press an edger between the forms and the concrete and guide it along the edge and the surface. Doing so produces rounded edges and helps prevent cracking. During the process, they help smooth the finish, wash away excess cement, and curve the surface with a special cement mixture. In addition to working with hand tools, such as trowels and edgers, concrete masons also use power-driven wheel barrels and concrete-leveling machines.

> **"Not everyone can be a concrete finisher. It's a fast-paced, strenuous job. It really keeps you in shape."**
> —Alise Martiny, cement mason

Bricklayers, who are also referred to as brick masons and block masons, build and repair walls, floors, fireplaces, and other structures made from bricks, blocks, and other masonry materials. Brick masons often use corner poles, or masonry guides, to build an entire wall at once. They define the wall line with a line stretched between two corner poles. Using a trowel, they spread a bed of mortar (a mix of cement, lime, sand, and water) and then press and tap each brick into place. Brick masons also use hammers, chisels, and saws to cut bricks so they fit around windows and doors.

Stonemasons keep track of their projects with drawings that show where each numbered stone goes. Helpers carry these stones to the masons, and if the stones are really big, a derrick operator actually hoists them into place. Stonemasons use wedges, plumblines, levelers, and hard rubber mallets to align and position the stones, and brackets to hold everything in place. They also work with other tools, including trowels, crowbars, and chisels.

Keys to Success

For success as a mason or concrete worker, you should have

- hand-eye coordination
- manual dexterity
- good balance
- physical fitness
- solid math skills
- team-playing ability

Do You Have What It Takes?

Whether you're pouring concrete, laying bricks, or building a stone wall, masonry work can be very demanding. You must be physically fit, have good hand-eye coordination, and enough endurance to work long days. Having good balance is crucial because you may need to work on a high scaffold or kneel for long periods of time. Because masons often work in fast-paced teams, they have to be able to work quickly and get along with others.

A Typical Day at Work

Because wind and temperature control how concrete sets, they also control the work life of a concrete mason or finisher. During the summer, a concrete finisher is in a race against time, especially on hot days when the concrete is in danger of setting too fast. To beat the sun, some workers start at the crack of dawn and don't even stop for lunch. While working, masons rely on their sense of sight and touch to catch and repair defects in the concrete.

Bricklayers and stonemasons work outdoors while building and repairing patios, walls, and other stone and brick structures. When placing the bricks and stones, they often have to stand, kneel, and bend for long stretches of time.

How to Break In

You can get a head start on your career plans by taking high school courses in math, mechanical drawing, and science. You also can pick up experience working as a helper with a concrete crew or by volunteering on a Habitat for Humanity building project.

Gaining experience as an apprentice is also crucial. Not only will you make money as an apprentice, but some apprenticeship sponsors will help cover your educational costs. For apprenticeship leads, try contacting local contractors and unions. Professional organizations, such as the National Concrete Masonry Association (http://www.ncma.org) and the American Concrete Institute (http://www.aci-int.org/general/home.asp), also can provide helpful information and contacts. Another good source is the U.S. Department of Labor, which provides information on apprenticeships with links to state programs (http://www.doleta.gov/OA/eta_default.cfm).

When you're in school and working as an apprentice, be sure to reach out to professional organizations in your field. Doing so will give you a better understanding of your chosen career and could help you land a job once your training is completed.

Two-Year Training

A two-year degree in masonry coupled with an apprenticeship can prepare you for a career as a mason.

Securing an apprenticeship through a local contractor, trade association, or local union can provide you with a chance to start earning money while you learn your trade from an experienced journeyman. Some apprenticeship sponsors will even help pay for your education.

Trainees usually start with simple assignments and are paid about half the rate of an experienced journeyman. For example, a beginning concrete mason apprentice might work as an assistant, mixing mortar or loading bricks or stones onto a scaffold. Apprentice brick masons often start as laborers who carry materials, mix the mortar, and build scaffolds. As an apprentice gains more experience, he or she gets to perform more skilled tasks, such as laying and joining bricks.

Training lasts three to four years and includes at least of 144 hours of classroom instruction. While in school, you'll have an opportunity to learn different specialties. Depending on your career path, you may learn how to lay bricks and build a fireplace, or learn how to work with cement and concrete.

You'll also learn to read drawings and blueprints, identify various building codes, and write industry reports. You'll learn how to identify different building materials and how they relate to each other structurally; and you'll take helpful academic courses, such as technical algebra and trigonometry.

What to Look For in a School

When considering a two-year school, be sure to ask these questions:

☞ Does the school offer related course work in subjects, such as site preparation and layout, and concrete block construction?

☞ Can the school help you find an apprenticeship where you can get on-the-job training?

☞ What is the school's job placement rate?

☞ What are the instructors' credentials? Have they worked in the industry?

☞ Does the school offer the tools needed for hands-on learning?

☞ Does the school offer management, finance, and other business classes for students who eventually want to start their own businesses?

The Future

With a crumbling infrastructure throughout the country, the demand for cement masons who can repair and build highways, bridges, and other structures will be high in the coming years. The demand for terrazzo workers, brick layers, and stone masons is also expected to exceed the supply of skilled workers, offering trained workers numerous opportunities in these fields.

Did You Know?

The world's largest concrete dam is the Grand Coulee Dam on the Columbia River in Washington State. According to Guinness World Records, it is 551 feet high and has a crest length of 4,173 feet.

Job Seeking Tips

See the suggestions below and turn to Appendix A for advice on creating a résumé, interviewing for schools or jobs, and collecting references.

✔ Decide what you're interested in and seek relevant experience.

✔ Seek advice from your school's career placement officer.

✔ Reach out and, when possible, join associations in your chosen field.

✔ Combine your educational training with an apprenticeship, in which you'll gain hands-on experience.

Interview with a Professional:
Q&A

Alise Martiny

President of Greater Kansas City Cement Masons
and Plasterers Union, Kansas City, Missouri

Q: *How did you get started?*

A: I went through a preapprenticeship program, which is six weeks of training. I successfully completed it and enrolled in a union apprentice program.

During the time you're in an apprentice program, you actually get to
work in the construction industry. You out go out and work in the field. The
journey people take you under their wings and mentor and teach you. During your down time, you go to school and learn safety rules and learn aspects of the industry that might not be the focus of your particular
contractor.

Q: *What's a typical day like?*

A: Being a concrete finisher, everything is always controlled by the weather.
On very hot days, the heat helps the concrete set faster, so we start at day-
light. Most crews start at 6 in the morning. In the winter months, we nor-
mally work from 8 to 4:30. In the summer, some crews start pouring at 3 in
the morning.

As a concrete finisher, every job is different. One day it might be 90,
where it'll set faster. One day it's cool and partly cloudy, and it sets differ-
ently.

Concrete is so perishable, so you work very quickly. Some days you
don't get a lunch break because the concrete is setting at such a fast pace. In
the winter months, you might be there for 20 hours because it's so cold that
it's not setting.

Q: *What's your advice for people starting a career?*

A: You've got to be there on time. You have to be able to work a full eight-
hour day where you don't get a lot of breaks. Yes, you'll be able to use the
bathroom and get a drink of water, but you don't really get the physical
time to stop and take a 30-minute break.

Q: *What's the best part about being a mason?*

A: The best part of the job is looking back and realizing how much you've
contributed to the community. You're not just working as a team to pour
the concrete. You're working with all types of different trades who are all
working together to build a city.

Career Connections

For more information about masonry careers, contact the following organizations.

National Concrete Masonry Association http://www.ncma.org

Associated Builders and Contractors, Workforce Development Division http://www.trytools.org

Associated General Contractors of America, Inc. http://www.agc.org

International Union of Bricklayers and Allied Craftworkers, International Masonry Institute http://www.imiweb.org

United Brotherhood of Carpenters and Joiners http://www.carpenters.org

Operative Plasterers' and Cement Masons' International Association of the United States and Canada http://www.opcmia.org

National Center for Construction Education and Research http://www.nccer.org

Portland Cement Association http://www.cement.org

American Concrete Institute http://www.aci-int.org/general/home.asp

Masonry training http://www.masonry-training.com

Associate's Degree Programs

Here are a few schools with two-year masonry programs:

Pennsylvania College of Technology, Williamsport, Pennsylvania

Wisconsin Indianhead Technical College, Rice Lake, Wisconsin

Alpena Community College (Concrete Technology Program), Alpena, Michigan

Southern Maine Community College, South Portland, Maine

Financial Aid

Here is a masonry-related scholarship. Turn to Appendix B for more on financial aid for two-year students.

Pennsylvania Concrete Masonry Association Scholarship goes to students majoring in the field of masonry.   http://www.pct.edu/scholarships/scholarships.htm#Pennsylvania%20Concrete%20Masonry%20Association%20

Related Careers

Concrete finisher, segmental paver, carpet floor and tile installer, drywall installer, ceiling title installer and paperer, plasterer, and stucco mason.

Marine Service Technician

Vital Statistics

Salary: The median hourly salary for marine service technicians is $14.74 an hour, or about $30,660 a year, according to the U.S. Bureau of Labor Statistics. Top earners make more than $45,600 a year.

Employment: The demand for marine service technicians is good, especially in areas in which boating is a year-round activity. The number of jobs in this field is expected to increase faster than the average for all occupations through 2014, according to the Bureau of Labor Statistics.

Education: A two-year degree in a marine service technician program coupled with on-the-job training will prepare you for a career in this field. While in school and at work as trainees, students learn how to service and repair boats with outboard and inboard engines. Because of the many different types of boats, and their multiple components, three to five years of training usually are needed before you're qualified to work on all kinds of repairs.

Work Environment: Because marine service technicians work on boats, they generally work on or near the water. Repairs are made inside repair shops and outside on boats in the water or on a trailer in the boatyard.

A boat gliding across the glistening water is so inviting. It's enough to make some people dream of finding a career in which they can work around boats and, if they're really lucky, on the water.

For water lovers who enjoy working with their hands, a career as a marine service technician can be a perfect match. Not only do marine service technicians get to work on engines, but their jobs often are located on or near the coast, a river, or a lake.

In the early spring, marine service mechanics rush to get customers' boats ready for the start of the boating season. They charge batteries, check engines, and perform other tasks. During the summer, they serve as troubleshooters—adjusting motors, fixing bilge pumps, and repairing steering systems. When fall comes, they pull boats out of the water and prepare them for winter storage.

Some marine technicians specialize, focusing on inboard engines, outboard motors, boat rigging, or electronic equipment. Others move into boat sales or service management.

To become a marine service technician, students often combine formal instruction at a community college or trade and technical school with on-the-job training at local marinas or boat dealerships. While working as trainees, students learn basic service tasks, such as how to replace ignition points and spark plugs. Boat makers also offer training programs for specific boat models. There's a lot to learn, so it can take a beginning mechanic several years before he or she is able to handle all kinds of repair work.

The workload for mechanics can be seasonal: Marine technicians in the northern regions of the country are incredibly busy in the spring and summer. Business tapers off a bit in the fall and then drops off dramatically in the winter.

The median salary for motorboat mechanics is about $30,660 a year, with top wage earners making more than $45,600 a year. For boat lovers, the biggest perk is getting to work around boats all day. For someone who loves the water, getting paid to test drive a boat is about as good as it gets.

On the Job

Marine service technicians maintain and repair everything from personal watercraft and ski boats to fishing vessels and sailboats. With so many different kinds of boats, a marine service technician's job is never boring. On one day, she or he may need to repair a manual starter or replace a water pump on a ski boat. On another day, the technician may be asked to rig a new sailboat, troubleshoot an electrical problem on a houseboat, or replace a bent propeller on a fishing boat.

To do their jobs, marine service technicians work with wrenches, pliers, drills, and a variety of other tools. They also use electronic gear, such as computerized engine analyzers, compression gauges, and voltmeters to find faulty parts, tune engines, and make other high-tech repairs.

During the spring, mechanics put in long days, rushing to get boats ready for the start of the new boating season. In the summer, they work at a fast pace so they can quickly get customers' "broken" boats back in the water. When winter approaches, technicians pull the boats out of the water and perform the protective maintenance needed to withstand the coming cold weather.

Keys to Success

To succeed in the marine service field you should have
- mechanical aptitude
- ability to work with hands
- creative problem-solving skills
- strong communication skills
- attention to detail

Do You Have What It Takes?

To be a marine service technician, you should enjoy working with your hands, have a mechanical aptitude, be a troubleshooter, and love working around boats. You'll need to be a good communicator who can write precise work orders and explain boat repairs to customers. Because technicians have to connect color-coded wires, you should also be able to differentiate among colors.

A Typical Day at Work

A marine service technician's day varies, depending on the time of the year and the tasks at hand. During the early spring, you get boats ready for the water: You clean the boat's hull, check its engine, hook up the battery, and perform other needed repairs.

Speed is essential, as customers are eager to get out on their boats as soon as the weather turns warm. During the summer, you become a troubleshooter. If a rock bends a propeller, you examine the propeller to see if it can be repaired or needs to be replaced. If a boat won't start, you check to see if the battery needs to be recharged or the starter needs to be repaired.

How to Break In

Believe it or not, you can get a jump on your career while still in high school. If you live near a marina, check to see if the marina hires extra workers during the busy summer months. Depending on your skills, the marina may put you to work gassing up boats, painting boat bottoms, assembling new equipment, and even performing minor repairs.

While you're still in high school, you can take courses that will help you master the skills you'll need as a marine service technician. Good choices include small engine repair, automobile mechanics, science, and business arithmetic.

After high school, enrollment in a two-year program at a community college or technical school that offers courses in marine mechanics is a smart move. Try to find a school that has a partnership with marinas and dealerships that provide on-the-job training. Not only will you learn valuable skills and earn money as a trainee, but your hard work could lead to a permanent job.

Two-Year Training

Students who want to be marine service technicians can learn the essentials in a two-year program that provides a mix of classroom instruction and hands-on training. Schools often have high-tech labs where students are given opportunities to diagnose and repair common problems and even take apart and rebuild systems.

While in school, you'll learn how to safely use required tools and equipment. You'll get to service, repair, and overhaul two- and four-stroke cycle marine engines, and outboard motors. You'll also learn how to work on electrical, fuel, power transfer, ignition, cooling, lubrication, and drive systems; and you'll learn how to rig, or set up, a boat and its trailer. Once you master the basics, you'll be ready to take more advanced courses that focus on repairs to products made by specific manufacturers.

Students who work as trainees at marinas and dealerships learn how to perform basic service tasks under the watchful eyes of experienced technicians. Generally, beginning mechanics need three to five years of training before they have enough experience to handle all kinds of repair work. Even then, the training never ends. Seasoned mechanics often attend manufacturers' schools to learn how to service and repair new products.

What to Look For in a School

When considering a two-year school, be sure to ask these questions:

☞ Does the school partner with local marinas or dealerships to provide on-the-job training?

☞ Does the school have a job placement office? What is it its job placement rate?

☞ Does the school have high-tech labs in which students can diagnose and repair common problems?

☞ What areas of specialization does the school offer? For example, does it offer specialized courses in which students learn how to service and repair products from specific manufacturers?

☞ What are the instructors' credentials? Do they have real-life experience? Are they available outside of the classroom?

☞ Is the school affiliated with or accredited by any professional associations, such as the American Boat & Yacht Council (http://www.abycinc.org/), the Association of Marine Technicians (http://www.am-tech.org/), or the Accrediting Commission of Career Schools and Colleges of Technology (http://www.accsct.org/)?

The Future

More people are expected to buy boats in the next decade, which means the demand for marine service technicians will probably continue to be strong. The best opportunities will go to marine service technicians with the most skills. Employees who can work on both two- and four-stroke engines will be in demand, as will those who understand emission-reducing technology.

Interview with a Professional:
Q&A

Eric Johansen

Service manager, Hinckley Yachts,
Oxford, Maryland

Q: *How did you get started?*

A: I've always had boats since I was a little kid. I am probably one of the very few kids who knew what I wanted to do for a living. Back when I was five, it was a sea captain. I've always had a passion for boats and knew I wanted to work on them. I had my own boats and was very curious how outboard motors worked. Much to my father's dismay, I would tear them apart and he would help me put them back together.

Q: *What's a typical day like?*

A: At the height of season in the spring, every morning we have a meeting with all the trade foremen. We have a mechanical foreman, a cleaning foreman, a painting foreman, a rigging foreman, a carpentry foreman. The first half hour of the day, we go over all the boats that have to be ready. It is an opportunity for service managers to tell the trades what needs to happen, to determine what needs to happen to get the boat out of here by next weekend.

When a boat is seaworthy again, the lift crew puts it back on the water, gets the batteries hooked up, gets the engine started, moves it to the slip and puts the sails on. When boats go away, they go away for an hour, a month, or all summer. When they come back with a problem—the engine's overheating, the toilet won't flush, the lights are out—that's our summer work.

Q: *What's your advice for those starting a career?*

A: No. 1. Have a skill. You need to be good at what you do.

No. 2. I think people have a natural talent for working with things like boats. Some guys are just mechanically able. Some guys are great boat handlers.

Q: *What's the best part of being a marine service technician?*

A: The greatest thing about being a mechanic is taking something that didn't work and making it work. One of the best highs is, if someone is stranded, we go out in a boat and bring them a battery. If you run out there with a battery or fuel filter and get the boat running, their gratitude is one of the greatest rewards. You've "saved their weekend."

Did You Know?

Boat owners often give their vessels names. The Boat U.S. Graphics Department, which makes custom boat graphics, keeps track of the most requested boat names. Recent favorites include Island Time, Hakuna Matata, Fish Tales, Liberty, Seas the Day, Freedom, and Summer Wind.

Job Seeking Tips

See the suggestions below and turn to Appendix A for tips on creating a résumé, interviewing for schools or jobs, and collecting references.

✔ Decide what you're interested in and seek relevant experience.

✔ Talk to your school's career placement officer.

✔ Reach out to, and if possible, join industry associations, such as the Association of Marine Technicians and the American Boat & Yacht Council.

Career Connections

For more information on a career as a marine technician, contact the following organizations.

American Boat & Yacht Council http://www.abycinc.org

Association of Marine Technicians http://www.am-tech.org

Accrediting Commission of Career Schools and Colleges of Technology http://www.accsct.org

National Marine Manufacturers Association http://www.nmma.org

> ## "You're never done with your training. Right about the time you think you've got it down, they change the technology."
> —Eric Johansen, marine technician

Associate's Degree Programs

Here are a few schools offering quality marine service technician programs:

The Landing School of Boat Building and Design, Kennebunkport, Maine

Wisconsin Indianhead Technical College, Ashland, Wisconsin

Carteret Community College, Morehead City, North Carolina
Lake Career and Technical Center, Camdenton, Missouri
H.B. Ward Technical Center, BOCES, Riverhead, New York

Financial Aid

Here are two scholarships in the field of marine service. Turn to Appendix B for more resources on financial aid for two-year students.

Universal Technical Institute (UTI) National Scholarship Competition awards scholarships to more than 380 students on its campuses, including those enrolled in the Marine Mechanics Institute in Orlando, Florida. http://www.uticorp.com/go/studentcenter/scholarships

Association of Marine Technicians awards the Harry Nowak Memorial Scholarship to students in approved marine service technician programs. http://www.am-tech.org

Related Careers

Motorcycle mechanic, lawn and garden equipment dealer, automotive service technician and mechanic, diesel service technician and mechanic, and heavy vehicle and mobile equipment service technician and mechanic.

Appendix A
Tools for Career Success

When 20-year-old Justin Schulman started job-hunting for a position as a fitness trainer—his first step toward managing a fitness facility—he didn't mess around. "I immediately opened the Yellow Pages and started calling every number listed under health and fitness, inquiring about available positions," he recalls. Schulman's energy and enterprise paid off: He wound up with interviews that led to several offers of part-time work.

Schulman's experience highlights an essential lesson for jobseekers: There are plenty of opportunities out there, but jobs won't come to you—especially the career-oriented, well-paying ones that that you'll want to stick with over time. You've got to seek them out.

Uncover Your Interests

Whether you're in high school or bringing home a full-time paycheck, the first step toward landing your ideal job is assessing your interests. You need to figure out what makes you tick. After all, there is a far greater chance that you'll enjoy and succeed in a career that taps into your passions, inclinations, and natural abilities. That's what happened with career-changer Scott Rolfe. He was already 26 when he realized he no longer wanted to work in the food industry. "I'm an avid outdoorsman," Rolfe says, "and I have an appreciation for natural resources that many people take for granted." Rolfe turned his passions into his ideal job as a forest technician.

If you have a general idea of what your interests are, you're far ahead of the game. You may know that you're cut out for a health care career, for instance, or one in business. You can use a specific volume of *Top Careers in Two Years* to discover what position to target. If you are unsure of your direction, check out the whole range of volumes to see the scope of jobs available. Ask yourself, what job or jobs would I most like to do if I *already* had the training and skills? Then remind yourself that this is what your two-year training will accomplish.

You can also use interest inventories and skills-assessment programs to further pinpoint your ideal career. Your school or public librarian or guidance counselor should be able to help you locate such assessments. Web sites such as America's Career InfoNet (http://www.acinet.org) and JobWeb (http://www.jobweb.com) also offer interest inventories. Don't forget the help advisers at any two-year college can provide to target your interests. You'll find suggestions for Web sites related to specific careers at the end of each chapter in any *Top Careers in Two Years* volume.

Unlock Your Network

The next stop toward landing the perfect job is networking. The word may make you cringe. But networking isn't about putting on a suit, walking into a roomful of strangers, and pressing your business card on everyone. Networking is simply introducing yourself and exchanging job-related and other information that may prove helpful to one or both of you. That's what Susan Tinker-Muller did. Quite a few years ago, she struck up a conversation with a fellow passenger on her commuter train. Little did she know that the natural interest she expressed in the woman's accounts payable department would lead to news about a job opening there. Tinker-Muller's networking landed her an entry-level position in accounts payable with MTV Networks. She is now the accounts payable administrator.

Tinker-Muller's experience illustrates why networking is so important. Fully 80 percent of openings are *never* advertised, and more than half of all employees land their jobs through networking, according to the U.S. Bureau of Labor Statistics. That's 8 out of 10 jobs that you'll miss if you don't get out there and talk with people. And don't think you can bypass face-to-face conversations by posting your résumé on job sites like Monster.com and Hotjobs.com and then waiting for employers to contact you. That's so mid-1990s! Back then, tens of thousands, if not millions, of job seekers diligently posted their résumés on scores of sites. Then they sat back and waited . . . and waited . . . and waited. You get the idea. Big job sites like Monster and Hotjobs have their place, of course, but relying solely on an Internet job search is about as effective as throwing your résumé into a black hole.

Begin your networking efforts by making a list of people to talk to: teachers, classmates (and their parents), anyone you've worked with, neighbors, worship acquaintances, and anyone you've interned or volunteered with. You can also expand your networking opportunities through the student sections of industry associations (listed at the end of each chapter of *Top Careers in Two Years*); attending or volunteering at industry events, association conferences, career fairs; and through job-shadowing. Keep in mind that only rarely will any of the people on your list be in a position to offer you a job. But whether they know it or not, they probably know someone who knows someone who is. That's why your networking goal is not to ask for a job but the name of someone to talk with. Even when you network with an employer, it's wise to say something like, "You may not have any positions available, but might you know someone I could talk with to find out more about what it's like to work in this field?"

Also, keep in mind that networking is a two-way street. For instance, you may be talking with someone who has a job opening that isn't appropriate for you. If you can refer someone else to the employer, either person may well be disposed to help you someday in the future.

Dial-Up Help

Call your contacts directly, rather than e-mail them. (E-mails are too easy for busy people to ignore, even if they don't mean to.) Explain that you're a recent graduate in your field; that Mr. Jones referred you; and that you're wondering if you could stop by for 10 or 15 minutes at your contact's convenience to find out a little more about how the industry works. If you leave this message as a voicemail, note that you'll call back in a few days to follow up. If you reach your contact directly, expect that they'll say they're too busy at the moment to see you. Ask, "Would you mind if I check back in a couple of weeks?" Then jot down a note in your date book or set up a reminder in your computer calendar and call back when it's time. (Repeat this above scenario as needed, until you get a meeting.)

Once you have arranged to talk with someone in person, prep yourself. Scour industry publications for insightful articles; having up-to-date knowledge about industry trends shows your networking contacts that you're dedicated and focused. Then pull together questions about specific employers and suggestions that will set you apart from the job-hunting pack in your field. The more specific your questions (for instance, about one type of certification versus another), the more likely your contact will see you as an "insider," worthy of passing along to a potential employer. At the end of any networking meeting, ask for the name of someone else who might be able to help you further target your search.

Get a Lift

When you meet with a contact in person (as well as when you run into someone fleetingly), you need an "elevator speech." This is a summary of up to two minutes that introduces who you are, as well as your experience and goals. An elevator speech should be short enough to be delivered during an elevator ride with a potential employer from the ground level to a high floor. In it, it's helpful to show that 1) you know the business involved; 2) you know the company; 3) you're qualified (give your work and educational information); and 4) you're goal-oriented, dependable, and hardworking. You'll be surprised how much information you can include in two minutes. Practice this speech in front of a mirror until you have the key points down very well. It should sound natural though, and you should come across as friendly, confident, and assertive. Remember, good eye contact needs to be part of your presentation as well as your everyday approach when meeting prospective employers or leads.

Get Your Résumé ready

In addition to your elevator speech, another essential job-hunting tool is your résumé. Basically, a résumé is a little snapshot of you in words, reduced to one 8½ x 11-inch sheet of paper (or, at most, two sheets). You need a résumé whether you're in high school, college, or the workforce, and whether you've never held a job or have had many.

At the top of your résumé should be your heading. This is your name, address, phone numbers, and your e-mail address, which can be a sticking point. E-mail addresses such as sillygirl@yahoo.com or drinkingbuddy @hotmail.com won't score you any points. In fact they're a turn-off. So if you dreamed up your address after a night on the town, maybe it's time to upgrade. (Similarly, these days potential employers often check Myspace sites, personal blogs, and Web pages. What's posted there has been known to cost candidates a job offer.)

The first section of your résumé is a concise Job Objective (e.g., "Entry-level agribusiness sales representative seeking a position with a leading dairy cooperative"). These days, with word-processing software, it's easy and smart to adapt your job objective to the position for which you're applying. An alternative way to start a résumé, which some recruiters prefer, is to re-work the Job Objective into a Professional Summary. A Professional Summary doesn't mention the position you're seeking, but instead focuses on your job strengths (e.g., "Entry-level agribusiness sales rep; strengths include background in feed, fertilizer, and related markets and ability to contribute as a member of a sales team"). Which is better? It's your call.

The body of a résumé typically starts with your Job Experience. This is a chronological list of the positions you've held (particularly the ones that will help you land the job you want). Remember: never, never any fudging. However, it is okay to include volunteer positions and internships on the chronological list, as long as they're noted for what they are.

Next comes your Education section. Note: It's acceptable to flip the order of your Education and Job Experience sections if you're still in high school or have gone straight to college and don't have significant work experience. Summarize the major courses in your degree area, any certifications you've achieved, relevant computer knowledge, special seminars, or other school-related experience that will distinguish you. Include your grade average if it's more than 3.0. Don't worry if you haven't finished your degree. Simply write that you're currently enrolled in your program (if you are).

In addition to these elements, other sections may include professional organizations you belong to and any work-related achievements, awards, or recognition you've received. Also, you can have a section for your interests, such as playing piano or soccer (and include any notable achievements regarding your interests, for instance, placed third in Midwest Regional Piano Competition). You should also note other special abilities, such as "Fluent in French" or "Designed own Web site." These sorts of activities will reflect well on you, whether or not they are job-related.

You can either include your references or simply note, "References upon Request." Be sure to ask your references permission to use their name and alert them to the fact that they may be contacted, before you include them on your résumé. For more information on résumé writing, check out Web sites such as http://www.resume.monster.com.

Craft Your Cover Letter

When you apply for a job either online or by mail, it's appropriate to include a cover letter. A cover letter lets you convey extra information about yourself that doesn't fit or isn't always appropriate in your résumé. For instance, in a cover letter, you can and should mention the name of anyone who referred you to the job. You can go into some detail about the reason you're a great match, given the job description. You also can address any questions that might be raised in the potential employer's mind (for instance, a gap in your résumé). Don't, however, ramble on. Your cover letter should stay focused on your goal: to offer a strong, positive impression of yourself and persuade the hiring manager that you're worth an interview. Your cover letter gives you a chance to stand out from the other applicants and sell yourself. In fact, 23 percent of hiring managers say a candidate's ability to relate his or her experience to the job at hand is a top hiring consideration, according to a Careerbuilder.com survey.

You can write a positive, yet concise cover letter in three paragraphs: An introduction containing the specifics of the job you're applying for; a summary of why you're a good fit for the position and what you can do for the company; and a closing with a request for an interview, contact information, and thanks. Remember to vary the structure and tone of your cover letter. For instance, don't begin every sentence with "I."

Ace Your Interview

Preparation is the key to acing any job interview. This starts with researching the company or organization you're interviewing with. Start with the firm, group, or agency's own Web site. Explore it thoroughly; read about their products and services, their history, and sales and marketing information.

Check out their news releases, links that they provide, and read up on or Google members of the management team to get an idea of what they may be looking for in their employees.

Sites such as http://www.hoovers.com enable you to research companies across many industries. Trade publications in any industry (such as *Food Industry News, Hotel Business,* and *Hospitality Technology*) are also available online or in hard copy at many college or public libraries. Don't forget to make a phone call to contacts you have in the organization to get an even better idea of the company culture.

Preparation goes beyond research, however. It includes practicing answers to common interview questions:

☞ *Tell me about yourself* (Don't talk about your favorite bands or your personal history; give a brief summary of your background and interest in the particular job area.)

☞ *Why do you want to work here?* (Here's where your research into the company comes into play; talk about the firm's strengths and products or services.)

☞ *Why should we hire you?* (Now is your chance to sell yourself as a dependable, trustworthy, effective employee.)

☞ *Why did you leave your last job?* (This is not a talk show. Keep your answer short; never bad-mouth a previous employer. You can always say something simply such as, "It wasn't a good fit, and I was ready for other opportunities.")

Rehearse your answers, but don't try to memorize them. Responses that are natural and spontaneous come across better. Trying to memorize exactly what you want to say is likely to both trip you up and make you sound robotic.

As for the actual interview, to break the ice, offer a few pleasant remarks about the day, a photo in the interviewer's office, or something else similar. Then, once the interview gets going, listen closely and answer the questions you're asked, versus making any other point that you want to convey. If you're unsure whether your answer was adequate, simply ask, "Did that answer the question?" Show respect, good energy, and enthusiasm, and be upbeat. Employers are looking for people who are enjoyable to be around, as well as good workers. Show that you have a positive attitude and can get along well with others by not bragging during the interview, overstating your experience, or giving the appearance of being too self-absorbed. Avoid one-word answers, but at the same time don't blather. If you're faced with a silence after giving your response, pause for a few seconds, and then ask, "Is there anything else you'd like me to add?" Never look at your watch or answer your cellphone during an interview.

Near the interview's end, the interviewer is likely to ask you if you have any questions. Make sure that you have a few prepared, for instance:

☞ *"Tell me about the production process."*

☞ *"What's your biggest short-term challenge?"*

☞ *"How have recent business trends affected the company?"*

☞ *"Is there anything else that I can provide you with to help you make your decision?"*

☞ *"When will you make your hiring decision?"*

During a first interview, never ask questions like, "What's the pay?" "What are the benefits?" or "How much vacation time will I get?"

Find the Right Look

Appropriate dressing and grooming is also essential to interviewing success. For business jobs and many other occupations, it's appropriate to come to an interview in a nice (not stuffy) suit. However, different fields have various dress codes. In the music business, for instance, "business casual" reigns for many jobs. This is a slightly modified look, where slacks and a jacket are just fine for a guy, and a nice skirt and blouse and jacket or sweater are acceptable for a woman. Dressing overly "cool" will usually backfire.

In general, watch all of the basics from the shoes on up (no sneakers or sandals, and no overly high heels or short skirts for women). Also avoid attention-getting necklines, girls. Keep jewelry and other "bling" to a minimum. Tattoos and body jewelry are becoming more acceptable, but if you can take out piercings (other than in your ear), you're better off. Similarly, unusual hairstyles or colors may bias an employer against you, rightly or wrongly. Make sure your hair is neat and acceptable (get a haircut?). Also go light on the makeup, self-tanning products, body scents, and other grooming agents. Don't wear a baseball cap or any other type of hat; and by all means, take off your sunglasses!

Beyond your physical appearance, you already know to be well bathed to minimize odor (leave your home early if you tend to sweat, so you can cool off in private), make good eye contact, smile, speak clearly using proper English, use good posture (don't slouch), offer a firm handshake, and arrive within five minutes of your interview. (If you're unsure of where you're going, "Mapquest" it and consider making a dry-run to the site so you won't be late.) First impressions can make or break your interview.

Remember Follow-Up

After your interview, send a thank you note. This thoughtful gesture will separate you from most of the other candidates. It demonstrates your ability to follow through, and it catches your prospective employer's attention one more time. In a 2005 Careerbuilder.com survey, nearly 15 percent of 650 hiring managers said they wouldn't hire someone who failed to send a thank you letter after the interview. Thirty-two percent say they would still consider the candidate, but would think less of him or her.

So do you hand write or e-mail the thank you letter? The fact is that format preferences vary. One in four hiring managers prefer to receive a thank you note in e-mail form only; 19 percent want the e-mail, followed up with a hard copy; 21 percent want a typed hard-copy only; and 23 percent prefer just a handwritten note. (Try to check with an assistant on the format your potential employer prefers.) Otherwise, sending an e-mail and a handwritten copy is a safe way to proceed.

Winning an Offer

There are no sweeter words to a job hunter than "We'd like to hire you." So naturally, when you hear them, you may be tempted to jump at the offer. *Don't*. Once an employer wants you, he or she will usually give you some time to make your decision and get any questions you may have answered. Now is the time to get specific about salary and benefits, and negotiate some of these points. If you haven't already done so, check out salary ranges for your position and area of the country on sites such as Payscale.com, Salary.com, and Salaryexpert.com (basic info is free; specific requests are not). Also, find out what sorts of benefits similar jobs offer. Then don't be afraid to negotiate in a diplomatic way. Asking for better terms is reasonable and expected. You may worry that asking the employer to bump up his offer may jeopardize your job, but handled intelligently, negotiating for yourself in fact may be a way to impress your future employer—and get a better deal for yourself.

After you've done all the hard work that successful job-hunting requires, you may be tempted to put your initiative into autodrive. However, the efforts you made to land your job-from clear communication to enthusiasm- are necessary now to pave your way to continued success. As Danielle Little, a human-resources assistant, says, "You must be enthusiastic and take the initiative. There is an urgency to prove yourself and show that you are capable of performing any and all related tasks. If your manager notices that you have potential, you will be given additional responsibilities, which will help advance your career." So do your best work on the job, and build your credibility. Your payoff will be career advancement and increased earnings.

Appendix B

Financial Aid

One major advantage of earning a two-year degree is that it is much less expensive than paying for a four-year school. Two years is naturally going to cost less than four, and two-year graduates enter the workplace and start earning a paycheck sooner than their four-year counterparts.

The latest statistics from the College Board show that average yearly total tuition and fees at a public two-year college is $2,191, compared to $5,491 at a four-year public college. That cost leaps to more than $21,000 on average for a year at a private four-year school.

With college costs relatively low, some two-year students overlook the idea of applying for financial aid at all. But the fact is, college dollars are available whether you're going to a trade school, community college, or university. About a third of all Pell Grants go to two-year public school students, and while two-year students receive a much smaller percentage of other aid programs, the funding is there for many who apply.

How Does Aid Work?

Financial aid comes in two basic forms: merit-based and need-based.

Merit-based awards are typically funds that recognize a particular talent or quality you may have, and they are given by private organizations, colleges, and the government. Merit-based awards range from scholarships for good writing to prizes for those who have shown promise in engineering. There are thousands of scholarships available for students who shine in academics, music, art, science, and more. Resources on how to get these awards are provided later in this chapter.

Need-based awards are given according to your ability to pay for college. In general, students from families that have less income and fewer assets receive more financial aid. To decide how much of this aid you qualify for, schools look at your family's income, assets, and other information regarding your finances. You provide this information on a financial aid form—usually the federal government's Free Application for Federal Student Aid (FAFSA). Based on the financial details you provide, the school of your choice calculates your Expected Family Contribution (EFC). This is the amount you are expected to pay toward your education each year.

Once your EFC is determined, a school uses this simple formula to figure out your financial aid package:

Cost of attendance at the school

- – Your EFC
- – Other outside aid (private scholarships)
- = Need

Schools put together aid packages that meet that need using loans, work-study, and grants.

Know Your School

When applying to a school, it's a good idea to find out their financial aid policy and history. Read over the school literature or contact the financial aid office and find out the following:

✔ *Is the school accredited?* Schools that are not accredited usually do not offer as much financial aid and are not eligible for federal programs.

✔ *What is the average financial aid package at the school?* The typical award size may influence your decision to apply or not.

✔ *What are all the types of assistance available?* Check if the school offers federal, state, private, or institutional aid.

✔ *What is the school's loan default rate?* The default rate is the percentage of students who took out federal student loans and failed to repay them on time. Schools that have a high default rate are often not allowed to offer certain federal aid programs.

✔ *What are the procedures and deadlines for submitting financial aid?* Policies can differ from school to school.

✔ *What is the school's definition of satisfactory academic progress?* To receive financial aid, you have to maintain your academic performance. A school may specify that you keep up at least a C+ or B average to keep getting funding.

✔ *What is the school's job placement rate?* The job placement rate is the percentage of students who find work in their field of study after graduating.

You'll want a school with a good placement rate so you can earn a good salary that may help you pay back any student loans you have.

Be In It to Win It

The key to getting the most financial aid possible is filling out the forms, and you have nothing to lose by applying. Most schools require that you file the FAFSA, which is *free* to submit, and you can even do it online. For more information on the FAFSA, visit the Web site at http://www.fafsa.ed.gov. If you have any trouble with the form, you can call 1-800-4-FED-AID for help.

To receive aid using the FAFSA, you must submit the form soon after January 1 prior to the start of your school year. A lot of financial aid is delivered on a first-come, first-served basis, so be sure to apply on time.

Filing for aid will require some work to gather your financial information. You'll need details regarding your assets and from your income tax forms, which include the value of all your bank accounts and investments. The form also asks if you have other siblings in college, the age of your parents, or if you have children. These factors can determine how much aid you receive.

Three to four weeks after you submit the FAFSA, you receive a document called the Student Aid Report (SAR). The SAR lists all the information you provided in the FAFSA and tells you how much you'll be expected to contribute toward school, or your Expected Family Contribution (EFC). It's important to review the information on the SAR carefully and make any corrections right away. If there are errors on this document, it can affect how much financial aid you'll receive.

The Financial Aid Package

Using information on your SAR, the school of your choice calculates your need (as described earlier) and puts together a financial aid package. Aid packages are often built with a combination of loans, grants, and work-study. You may also have won private scholarships that will help reduce your costs.

Keep in mind that aid awarded in the form of loans has to be paid back with interest just like a car loan. If you don't pay back according to agreed upon terms, you can go into *default*. Default usually occurs if you've missed payments for 180 days. Defaulted loans are often sent to collection agencies, which can charge costly fees and even take money owed out of your wages. Even worse, a defaulted loan is a strike on your credit history. If you have a negative credit history, lenders may deny you a mortgage, car loan, or other personal loan. There's also financial incentive for paying back on time—many lenders will give a 1 percent discount or more for students who make consecutive timely payments. The key is not to borrow more than you can afford. Know exactly how much your monthly payments will be on a loan when it comes due and estimate if those monthly payments will fit in your future budget. If you ever do run into trouble with loan payments, don't hesitate to contact your lender and see if you can come up with a new payment arrangement—lenders want to help you pay rather than see you go into default. If you have more than one loan, look into loan consolidation, which can lower overall monthly payments and sometimes lock in interest rates that are relatively low.

The Four Major Sources of Aid

U.S. Government Financial Aid

The federal government is the biggest source of financial aid. To find all about federal aid programs, visit http://www.studentaid.fed.gov or call 1-800-4-FED-AID with any questions. Download the free brochure *Funding Education Beyond High School,* which tells you all the details on federal programs. To get aid from federal programs you must be a regular student working toward a degree or certificate in an eligible program. You also have to have a high school diploma or equivalent, be a U.S. citizen or eligible noncitizen and have a valid Social Security number (check http://www.ssa.gov for info). If you are a male aged 18–25, you have to register for the Selective Service. (Find out more about that requirement at http://www.sss.gov or call 1-847-688-6888.) You must also certify that you are not in default on a student loan and that you will use your federal aid only for educational purposes.

Some specifics concerning federal aid programs can change a little each year, but the major programs are listed here and the fundamentals stay the same from year to year. (Note that amounts you receive generally depend on your enrollment status—whether it be full-time or part-time.)

Pell Grant

For students demonstrating significant need, this award has been ranging between $400 and $4,050. The size of a Pell grant does not depend on how much other aid you receive.

Supplemental Educational Opportunity Grant (SEOG)

Again for students with significant need, this award ranges from $100 to $4,000 a year. The size of the SEOG can be reduced according to how much other aid you receive.

Work-Study

The Federal Work-Study Program provides jobs for students showing financial need. The program encourages community service and work related to a student's course of study. You earn at least minimum wage and are paid at least once a month. Again, funds must be used for educational expenses.

Perkins Loans
With a low interest rate of 5 percent, this program lets students who can document the need borrow up to $4,000 a year.

Stafford Loans
These loans are available to all students regardless of need. However, students with need receive *subsidized* Staffords, which do not accrue interest while you're in school or in deferment. Students without need can take *unsubsidized* Staffords, which do accrue interest while you are in school or in deferment. Interest rates vary but can go no higher than 8.25 percent. Loan amounts vary too, according to what year of study you're in and whether you are financially dependent on your parents or not. Students defined as independent of their parents can borrow much more. (Students who have their own kids are also defined as independent. Check the exact qualifications for independent and dependent status on the federal government Web site http://www.studentaid.fed.gov.)

PLUS Loans
These loans for parents of dependent students are also available regardless of need. Parents with good credit can borrow up to the cost of attendance minus any other aid received. Interest rates are variable but can go no higher than 9 percent.

Tax Credits
Depending on your family income, qualified students can take federal tax deductions for education with maximums ranging from $1,500 to $2,000.

AmeriCorps
This program provides full-time educational awards in return for community service work. You can work before, during, or after your postsecondary education and use the funds either to pay current educational expenses or to repay federal student loans. Americorps participants work assisting teachers in Head Start, helping on conservation projects, building houses for the homeless, and doing other good works. For more information, visit http://www.AmeriCorps.gov

State Financial Aid

All states offer financial aid, both merit-based and need-based. Most states use the FAFSA to determine eligibility, but you'll have to contact your state's higher education agency to find out the exact requirements. You can get contact information for your state at http://www.bcol02.ed.gov/Programs/EROD/org_list.cfm. Most of the state aid programs are available only if you study at a school in the state where you reside. Some states are very generous, especially if you're attending a state college or university. California's Cal Grant program gives needy state residents free tuition at in-state public universities.

School-Sponsored Financial Aid

The school you attend may offer its own loans, grants, and work programs. Many have academic- or talent-based scholarships for top-performing students. Some two-year programs offer cooperative education opportunities where you combine classroom study with off-campus work related to your major. The work gives you hands-on experience and some income, ranging from $2,500 to $15,000 per year depending on the program. Communicate with your school's financial aid department and make sure you're applying for the most aid you can possibly get.

Private Scholarships

While scholarships for students heading to four-year schools may be more plentiful, there are awards for the two-year students. Scholarships reward students for all sorts of talent—academic, artistic, athletic, technical, scientific, and more. You have to invest time hunting for the awards that you might qualify for. The Internet now offers many great scholarship search services. Some of the best ones are:

The College Board (http://www.collegeboard.com/pay)

FastWeb! (http://www.fastweb.monster.com)

MACH25 (http://www.collegenet.com)

Scholarship Research Network (http://www.srnexpress.com)

SallieMae's College Answer (http://www.collegeanswer.com)

Note: Be careful of scholarship-scam services that charge a fee for finding you awards but end up giving you nothing more than a few leads that you could have gotten for free with a little research on your own. Check out the Federal Trade Commission's Project ScholarScam (http://www.ftc.gov/bcp/conline/edcams/scholarship).

In your hunt for scholarship dollars, be sure to look into local community organizations (the Elks Club, Lions Club, PTA, etc.), local corporations, employers (your employer or your parents' may offer tuition assistance), trade groups, professional associations (National Electrical Contractors Association, etc.), clubs (Boy Scouts, Girl Scouts, Distributive Education Club of America, etc.), heritage organizations (Italian, Japanese,

Chinese, and other groups related to ethnic origin), church groups, and minority assistance programs.

Once you find awards you qualify for, you have to put in the time applying. This usually means filling out an application, writing a personal statement, and gathering recommendations.

General Scholarships

A few general scholarships for students earning two-year degrees are

Coca-Cola Scholars Foundation, Inc.
Coca-Cola offers 350 thousand-dollar scholarships (http://www.coca colascholars.org) per year specifically for students attending two-year institutions.

Phi Theta Kappa (PTK)
This organization is the International Honor Society of the Two-Year College. PTK is one of the sponsors of the All-USA Academic Team program, which annually recognizes 60 outstanding two-year college students (http://scholarships.ptk.org). First, Second, and Third Teams, each consisting of 20 members, are selected. The 20 First Team members receive stipends of $2,500 each. All 60 members of the All-USA Academic Team and their colleges receive extensive national recognition through coverage in *USA TODAY*. There are other great scholarships for two-year students listed on this Web site.

Hispanic Scholarship Fund (HSF)
HSF's High School Scholarship Program (http://www.hsf.net/scholar ship/programs/hs.php) is designed to assist high school students of Hispanic heritage obtain a college degree. It is available to graduating high school seniors who plan to enroll full-time at a community college during the upcoming academic year. Award amounts range from $1,000 to $2,500.

The Military
All branches of the military offer tuition dollars in exchange for military service. You have to decide if military service is for you. The Web site http://www.myfuture.com attempts to answer any questions you might have about military service.

Lower Your Costs

In addition to getting financial aid, you can reduce college expenses by being a money-smart student. Here are some tips.

Use Your Campus

Schools offer perks that some students never take advantage of. Use the gym. Take in a school-supported concert or movie night. Attend meetings and lectures with free refreshments.

Flash Your Student ID

Students often get discounts at movies, museums, restaurants, and stores. Always be sure to ask if there is a lower price for students and carry your student ID with you at all times. You can often save 10 to 20 percent on purchases.

Budget Your Funds

Writing a budget of your income and expenses can help you be a smart spender. Track what you buy on a budget chart. This awareness will save you dollars.

Share Rides

Commuting to school or traveling back to your hometown? Check and post on student bulletin boards for ride shares.

Buy Used Books

Used textbooks can cost half as much as new. Check your campus bookstore for deals and also try http://www.eCampus.com and http://www.bookcentral.com

Put Your Credit Card in the Freezer

That's what one student did to stop overspending. You can lock your card away any way you like, just try living without the ease of credit for awhile. You'll be surprised at the savings.

A Two-Year Student's Financial Aid Package

Minnesota State Colleges and Universities provides this example of how a two-year student pays for college. Note how financial aid reduces his out-of-pocket cost to about $7,000 per year.

Jeremy's Costs for One Year

Jeremy is a freshman at a two-year college in the Minnesota. He has a sister in college, and his parents own a home but have no other significant savings. His family's income: $42,000.

College Costs for One Year

Tuition	$3,437
Fees	$388
Estimated room and board*	$7,200
Estimated living expenses**	$6,116
Total cost of attendance	*$17,141*

Jeremy's Financial Aid

Federal grants (does not require repayment)	$2,800
Minnesota grant (does not require repayment)	$676
Work-study earnings	$4,000
Student loan (requires repayment)	$2,625
Total financial aid	*$10,101*
Total cost to Jeremy's family	*$7,040*

* Estimated cost reflecting apartment rent rate and food costs. The estimates are used to calculate the financial aid. If a student lives at home with his or her parents, the actual cost could be much less, although the financial aid amounts may remain the same.

** This is an estimate of expenses including transportation, books, clothing, and social activities.

Index